Inquiry Illuminated

Inquiry Illuminated
Researcher's Workshop Across the Curriculum

Anne Goudvis • Stephanie Harvey • Brad Buhrow
with *Karen Halverson*

Photography by **Ehren Joseph**

HEINEMANN

PORTSMOUTH, NH

Heinemann
145 Maplewood Ave., Suite 300
Portsmouth, NH 03801
www.heinemann.com

Offices and agents throughout the world

The authors and publisher wish to thank those who have generously given permission to reprint borrowed material:

Adapted from "Inquiry Approach vs. Coverage Approach" from *Comprehension and Collaboration: Inquiry Circles for Curiosity, Engagement, and Understanding,* Revised Edition, by Stephanie Harvey and Harvey "Smokey" Daniels. Copyright © 2009, 2015 by Stephanie Harvey and Harvey Daniels. Published Heinemann, Portsmouth, NH. Reprinted by permission of the Publisher. All Rights Reserved.

Acknowledgments for borrowed material continue on p. 253.

Cataloging-in-Publication Data is on file at the Library of Congress.
978-0-325-07790-1

Editor: Tina Miller and Heather Anderson
Production: Vicki Kasabian
Cover and interior designs: Monica Ann Crigler
Typesetter: Monica Ann Crigler
Manufacturing: Steve Bernier

Printed in the United States of America on acid-free paper
4 5 6 7 VP 26 25 24 23 22

"It may be that our cosmic curiosity . . . is a genetically encoded force that we illuminate when we look up and wonder."

—Neil DeGrasse Tyson

To all the fearless and thoughtful teachers and kids who are willing to wonder and learn with us.

Greetings friends,

Welcome to our newest resource, *Inquiry Illuminated: Researcher's Workshop Across the Curriculum*. This book shines a light on inquiry-based teaching and learning. For us, inquiry is not merely about an end product but rather a way of life. Curiosity is its lifeblood, where kids' questions matter. We've found that when we immerse kids in compelling content and share an inquiry process that teaches them how to do research and ultimately take the helm, they can't resist learning and diving deeper.

In recent years, we have noticed that too often science and social studies end up on the back burner. We believe it's high time to change that. How about we dedicate time to teach all content areas in a way that reflects the rich, textured, intriguing nature of these disciplines?

We love reader's and writer's workshop, so why not researcher's workshop? In a workshop model, kids get to do the reading, writing, and thinking. So, we advocate teaching content—science, social studies, language arts (and language arts is a jam-packed content area) in what we call *researcher's workshop*. Whether it's kids observing nesting birds on webcams, piecing together information about prehistoric fossils, reading about how to beautify a neighborhood, or taking action to convince college students to vote, all of which are described within, *researcher's workshop* gives kids the time and space to read, write, draw, talk, listen, view, create, and investigate.

In this book, we share examples of curricular inquiries in primary and intermediate grades. We understand that you have your own curriculum to explore and it is unlikely that you will be teaching the same content as in these examples. Our intent is to illuminate the research process with compelling curricular content so that you can apply it to your own curriculum. We include generic inquiry frameworks to support you to do just that.

Too often when we set out to "do inquiry," chaos reigns and we end up with more traditional research projects such as state, animal, or country reports. To counter this, we have designed a scaffolded inquiry process that provides accessible entry points for engaging in and following through with authentic research. We share a gradual-release framework for both students and teachers. We launch the inquiry process by modeling how we think and become researchers. We gradually move to guided inquiry, where kids take on more responsibility for and ownership of the process and teachers act as a "guide by the side." When we are confident that kids have the tools to research independently, we send them off and weigh in as needed. We teachers benefit from this gradual-release approach to inquiry as well. We are less likely to resort to more conventional research when the inquiry process is scaffolded like this.

As with much of our work, building knowledge through comprehension is at the foundation. Comprehension instruction is central to the many reading, writing, and research lessons and practices featured in this book. With comprehension at the core, inquiry leads kids to a deeper, more expanded understanding of the world. Renowned inquiry advocate Kath Murdoch (2015) reminds us that inquiry teachers and learners

> are driven by the desire not to simply accumulate or
> conquer a body of knowledge but to make meaning of
> the ever-changing knowledge landscape of which we
> are part. This includes acquiring knowledge, but it is
> understanding that is the ultimate quest. (17)

We are delighted that you have chosen to join us as we explore this quest.

Warmly,
Anne, Steph, Brad, and Karen

Contents

Creating a Culture for Inquiry *1*

To build a culture for inquiry in our classrooms, six cornerstones foster spirited, thoughtful learning: curiosity, workshop, content, comprehension, collaboration, and environment. These provide a strong foundation for inquiry at every grade level and across the curriculum.

Researcher's Workshop *41*

Enter Brad Buhrow's classroom to see how the cornerstones come to life in researcher's workshop. We introduce eleven core practices and lessons to teach the research process. We launch the inquiry process with whole-class research and gradually release kids to take more responsibility for the process. Finally kids take off on their own, confident as they use their repertoire of comprehension strategies and research tools to investigate their questions and interests.

Reading and Writing in Support of Inquiry *109*

In this chapter, you'll find more than twenty additional lessons and practices that are essential tools for readers, writers, and researchers. We often introduce these in reader's and writer's workshop, but students use them throughout the day and across the curriculum as they read, write, talk, listen, create, and investigate.

Inquiry Across the Grades *175*

Peek into classrooms where researcher's workshop is central to learning. Examples of inquiries in science, language arts, and social studies in grades one through four will spark your own ideas for inquiries with your curriculum. Inquiries featured here include investigating various cultures, learning to think like scientists, and exploring different perspectives in history.

Inquiry Across the Curriculum *211*

Weaving together literature, poetry, social studies, and history, intermediate teacher Karen Halverson describes how reading, writing, discussion, personal reflection, and creative expression come to life when kids tackle issues involving social justice and historical and cultural perspectives. With a firm foundation in the research process, inquiry is a way of life for these fifth graders.

Video Links

See inquiry in action with these snapshots of classroom instruction during researcher's workshop. Video clips are featured throughout the book to share specific lessons and practices and to illustrate the inquiry process across different grade levels and content areas.

▶ Researcher's Workshop

Revisit and discuss essential questions and enduring understandings.
Present information and take it public.
Get started with independent research.
Record important information and thinking.

▶ Reading and Writing in Support of Inquiry

Share and talk about books.
Observe, wonder, and learn about real stuff.
Use observations and websites to create field notes.
Watch a child teach how to record field notes.
Explore and share ways to write to inform.
Share a field guide.
Introduce design techniques.

▶ Inquiry Across the Grades

Research an essential question. (Second grade)
Create "thick" and "thin" questions for research. (Third grade)
Read, analyze, and discuss historical sources to understand multiple perspectives. (Fourth grade)
Engage in Socratic seminar to deepen understanding. (Fourth grade)

▶ Inquiry Across the Curriculum

Teacher and students reflect on poetry and performance.
Students perform slam poetry.

Video Access

Visit **http://hein.pub/ii-login** to access the online videos and online resources.

Enter your email address and password (or click "Create an Account" to set up an account). Once you have logged in, enter keycode **inquiry!** and click "Register." The landing page contains all the video clips. The video is listed by chapter.

Acknowledgments

This book came to fruition over many months with a veritable village of people contributing.

Lisa Fowler first inspired us to think about a book focused on kids' thinking, creative expression, and research—as she watched it all happening in Brad's classroom. We deeply appreciate her belief in our work.

Editor extraordinaire Tina Miller often knew what we wanted to say before we did. We are so grateful you came on this journey with us, but if we have anything to say about it, you still can't retire. Heather Anderson, unfailingly energetic and cheerful, provided thoughtful feedback on every photo and word, and at the same time, kept us moving forward. We couldn't have done it without you.

Photographer Ehren Joseph's creative eye and ability to make photo shoots fun for everyone captured life in these classrooms. We are grateful beyond words for his willingness to drop everything and come take "just a few more photos."

Virtually the entire K–5 staff at Columbine Elementary School in Boulder, Colorado, collaborated with us. After all these years together, we continue to learn so much from you every day. A special thanks to: Marisol Payet, Yolanda Perez, Melanie Pappageorge, Erin Livingston, Olivia Foulkrod, Anne Upczak Garcia, and Silvia Lattimer. Jeanette Scotti and Melissa Oviatt are teacher-librarians who live the idea that the library is the beating heart of any school. Principals Guillermo Medina and Bianca Gallegos always welcomed us and our numerous photo and video shoots with enthusiasm.

At Heinemann, designer Monica Crigler worked magic with hundreds of photos and thousands of words, so that kids' ideas and thinking shine through on every page.

The commitment and thoughtful expertise of the production team—Vicki Kasabian, Patty Adams, Michael Grover, and Sarah Fournier—made it all happen. In video and social media, Sherry Day and Brett Whitmarsh, along with Eric Chalek in marketing, turned their expertise and savvy media skills to taking this work public.

Over the years, we have been fortunate to be guided by the extraordinary leadership of Vicki Boyd and now Roderick Spelman. We thank them both for their commitment to publishing important, thoughtful work for teachers.

We thank our families, who, as always, provide both encouragement and welcome distractions. Kai Sionas, a fourth-grade teacher who happens to be Anne's son, happily provided thoughtful feedback at any time, day or night.

Above all, we thank the kids who inspire us every day and made this project come to life.

Creating a Culture for Inquiry

• •

"My best teachers taught me most by the way they inquired about the world, toyed with ideas, and expressed their convictions."

—Donald Graves

One day, Cooper and Tony, two rambunctious kindergartners with a penchant for animal life Down Under, headed back from the library, their arms overladen with marsupial books. As they scanned the classroom for an empty table, they saw the only available space was in the Home Living center. They quickly set up shop and dug in to photographs of koalas, kangaroos, and echidnas, jotting questions on Post-its and drawing their new learning. When someone entered the space to "make dinner and do the dishes," they graciously warded him off and then created and posted a sign at the entrance. So long, Home Living!

Just a few months into kindergarten, Tony and Cooper understood that their teacher honored their curiosity and encouraged their questions. So they took matters in their own hands, comfortable in a classroom that encourages independence, to carve out a place where they could explore and wonder.

Making a Case for Inquiry

As Tony and Cooper demonstrate, engaged, curious, active kids expand their understanding, build their knowledge, and embrace a desire to learn more. In classrooms that are built around an inquiry stance, teachers support kids to

> - live a life full of wonder and curiosity
> - explore topics, ideas, and issues that are central to their interests and concerns, linking these to the wider world
> - tackle big ideas, essential questions, and enduring understandings as they read, write, and research
> - use comprehension strategies flexibly to turn information into knowledge and actively use it
> - read and respond critically with an inquisitive mind and a skeptical stance
> - interact with text, media, resources, artifacts, teachers, and one another
> - research a vast array of topics of interest and importance
> - make thinking visible to demonstrate understanding
> - bathe content learning in rich talk and discussion
> - think creatively to express and share new learning
> - engage in collaborative inquiry and action.

The teachers in this book weave these practices throughout their teaching every day. In planning our inquiries, we account for topics, skills, and content that stem from district and state curriculum and standards as well as from kids' individual passions and curiosities. In conventional content instruction, "coverage" of the subject matter has been the goal. In inquiry-based classrooms, deep, meaningful learning—and sometimes action—is our mission. We discourage what we call a curriculum of "mentioning," covering facts and information in a cursory way. Instead, we center inquiry around content-related big ideas, essential questions, and enduring understandings, and connect these with real-world, real-life issues. In classrooms like these, kids burst with enthusiasm and energy for learning and wondering. They can't resist taking learning into their own hands as Cooper and Tony did when they switched out the Home Living center for a research lab. Student agency and independent thinking thrive when kids are passionate about a topic, and we encourage them all the way.

Inquiry Approach	vs.	Coverage Approach
Question/problem driven		Assignment driven
Student voice and choice		Teacher selection and direction
Interaction and talk		Quiet and listening
Student responsibility		Student compliance
Authentic investigations		Teacher presentations
Purposeful learning		Getting a grade
Collaborative work		Solitary work
Strategic thinking		Memorization
Cross-disciplinary issues		One subject at a time
Multiple resources		Reliance on a textbook
Multimodal learning		Verbal sources only
Using tools/procedures of a discipline		Hearing the findings of a discipline
Student as knowledge creator		Student as information receiver
Teacher as model and coach		Teacher as expert and presenter
Caring and taking action		Forgetting and moving to the next unit
Performance-based assessments		Classroom and standardized tests

(Adapted from Harvey and Daniels 2015)

Inquiry with Researcher's Workshop

In inquiry-based classrooms, researcher's workshop happens each and every day. Just as with reader's and writer's workshops, researcher's workshop is carefully structured and includes explicit instruction in research strategies and the inquiry process. In addition, researcher's workshop

- provides an authentic, practical context for reading, writing, drawing, talking, listening, and creating
- fosters personal engagement and ownership for every kid
- encourages kids to build knowledge as they use reading, writing, and thinking strategies in the service of learning.

During researcher's workshop, we sometimes focus our inquiries on topics that are part of a district-mandated curriculum unit. At other times we might explore a common topic, driven by kids, that's of particular local or current interest. The inquiries shared in this book are primarily curricular in nature but with plenty of room for kids to investigate on their own. When it comes to curricular inquiries, some may extend over several weeks. To make sure kids have enough time to explore their topics in depth, often teachers alternate science and social studies. They may spend two or three weeks on a science unit and the next few weeks on social studies. Others may integrate teaching science and social studies together. But either way, kids need plenty of time to read, write, and think about content to build knowledge and actively use it.

Flexible Inquiry Framework

The inquiry framework on the following pages demonstrates what teachers and students may do during each phase of the process. It's important to note that the inquiry phases are recursive, not linear. We may spend a week on immersion and move into investigation, only to circle back to more immersion. For instance, kids ask questions during the immerse phase. During coalesce, they can't resist taking their learning public. The purpose of this framework is merely to show the overall progression of kid-centered research. Once kids have internalized the routines and practices in the framework, they have their own blueprint for how to find things out. These are real-life, twenty-first-century strategies that kids will use for years to come. Just ask their parents.

As one second-grade parent commented when visiting his child's classroom, "As a scientist, this is exactly what I do all day, every day. I ask some questions, do some reading to find out what I need to know, write it up, and then share it with colleagues. It's just like what's happening in this classroom."

Inquiry Framework for Primary Grades

Inquiry units follow this four-phase learning sequence—Immerse, Investigate, Coalesce, and Take Public. Here you see the big picture. To make the inquiry process more accessible to teachers and kids, we take a gradual response approach described in the next chapter about researcher's workshop.

STAGE I. IMMERSE	Invite curiosity, build background, find topics
Teacher	**Students**
• Connect curriculum topics to kids' interests and experiences • Collect and organize resources: picture books, photos, trade books, artifacts, charts, magazines, and online sources • Immerse kids in topic and encourage questions and responses	• Connect new information to their background knowledge, lives, and experiences • Explore, experience, and learn about the topic using texts, visuals, and artifacts related to the topic • Listen, read, talk, view, draw, and write to respond and wonder

STAGE II. INVESTIGATE	Develop questions, search for information, and discover answers
Teacher	**Students**
• Demonstrate ways to read, view, and wonder about information • Show how to merge thinking with new information • Model learning from visual and text features • Demonstrate how to ask and answer questions	• Read, write, talk, and draw to wonder about new information • React, respond, and merge their thinking as they learn new information • Notice and record information from features • Develop questions and read/view to answer them

STAGE III. COALESCE	Intensify research, synthesize information, and build knowledge
Teacher	**Students**
• Teach paraphrasing information • Show how to infer and visualize ideas and information • Show ways to summarize information and add your thinking • Connect student learning to enduring understandings and essential questions	• Put information into own words to understand it • Infer and visualize from a variety of features and in different genres • Express learning in original ways • Come to their own understandings of EUs and EQs

STAGE IV. TAKE PUBLIC	Share learning, demonstrate understanding and new insights. Take action
Teacher	**Students**
• Establish expectations for projects and ways to respond to and assess them • Model possibilities for final projects and ways to take action • Help kids articulate their learning process • Provide opportunities for kids to respond to one another's work to build a community of learners	• Demonstrate understanding and learning through writing and drawing posters, digital texts, picture books, and so on • Become teachers as they share knowledge with others through projects • Come to care about their learning and take action

(Adapted from Harvey and Daniels 2015)

Inquiry Framework for Intermediate Grades

Researcher's workshop, the teaching scaffold for content-area inquiries, is built on this inquiry framework.

STAGE I. IMMERSE   Invite curiosity, build background, find topics

Teacher	Students
• Plan instruction and teach with central concepts and focus questions in mind	• Read, write, talk, listen, observe in small groups, partners, large groups, and independently
• Gather and organize materials (trade books, picture books, articles, photographs, videos, websites)	• Turn and talk in response to instruction
• Engage kids in interactive read-alouds	• Get engaged and develop familiarity with the topic
• Model personal responses, demonstrate strategy use, and share thinking	• Acquire vocabulary and concepts
• Demonstrate leaving tracks of thinking and note-taking	• Access background knowledge and react to information with questions, connections, and the like
• Immerse kids in picture book clubs	• Read picture/trade books and record information, questions, and responses

STAGE II. INVESTIGATE   Develop questions, search for information, and discover answers

Teacher	Students
• Model reading and thinking with texts that focus on unit-of-study concepts	• Read, write, talk, and think about information
• Demonstrate how to ask and answer questions	• Read to find the answers to their questions
• Demonstrate a variety of techniques to access information and respond to it	• Read, gather, and respond to information that interests them
◆ Coding text to hold thinking	• Use evidence and information to distinguish between reader's thinking and author's thinking
◆ Note-taking	• Practice all the above strategies and techniques in large groups, in small groups, with partners, and independently
◆ Using text features to gain information	• Develop questions and read to address them
◆ Leaving tracks of thinking on Post-its and response forms	
• Develop focus questions and read with a question in mind	

STAGE III. COALESCE Intensify research, synthesize information, and build knowledge	
Teacher	**Students**
Model instruction to: ● Develop focus questions and read with a question in mind ● Gather details and text evidence that support bigger ideas ● Infer answers to questions that aren't answered in the text ● Show how to read to get the gist ● Summarize and synthesize information in a variety of ways ● Connect student learning to enduring understandings and essential questions	● Develop questions and read to answer them ● Use text evidence to infer the answers to questions that aren't answered ● Seek out additional sources to address unaddressed questions ● Use evidence and details to support big ideas ● Read to get the gist ● Develop their own take on EUs and EQs

STAGE IV. TAKE PUBLIC Share learning, demonstrate understanding and new insights. Take action	
Teacher	**Students**

● Establish the expectations for sharing
● Suggest ways kids might share their learning and take it public. Possibilities include but are not limited to the following:
    ◆ Summary responses—Short responses (one or two pages) that merge the information learned with the writer's thinking
    ◆ Teaching posters—Posters that summarize learning and teach new information through writing and illustrations
    ◆ First-person journals, diaries, and letters—Accounts, written from one person's perspective that weave together information and historical narrative
    ◆ Picture books—Informational books and narrative nonfiction that teach about a certain topic
    ◆ Question webs—Group webs where kids collaborate to answer related questions
    ◆ Newspaper, magazine, and online articles—Journalistic accounts that summarize information, including the bigger ideas
    ◆ Essays—Written pieces about ideas, issues, and perspectives
    ◆ Videos—Media projects that synthesize the information
    ◆ Wikis—Online multimedia platforms for sharing writing, voice, and art
    ◆ PowerPoint slides—Digital capsules of information for oral presentations
    ◆ Digital books—Online informational or narrative summaries
	● Create projects that demonstrate their learning and understanding, either those suggested by teachers or those they think of themselves
	● Become teachers as they take their thinking public and share their new knowledge with others
	● Articulate their learning process and reflect on it
	● Discover and consider new questions spurred by sharing with each other
	● Take ownership of what they are learning, come to care about it, and take action

Six Cornerstones of Inquiry

We subscribe to Vygotsky's idea that "children grow into the intellectual life around them" (1978, 88). It's on us to create an environment for inquiry that inspires kids to explore, investigate, and want to learn more. Six cornerstones that foster this kind of active, spirited, all-in learning include

- Curiosity
- Workshop
- Content
- Comprehension
- Collaboration
- Classroom environment

In the following pages, we share our vision for how these cornerstones create and shape the classroom environment, and include specific practices that encourage each of these.

Cornerstone 1. Curiosity

E. B. White reminds us to "always be on the lookout for the presence of wonder." When kids know their thinking and ideas matter, wondering is irresistible. In the classroom discovery center, kids scour recent articles about a dinosaur discovered just a few miles away. They preview an online newscast and read about the Torosaurus, sharing this exciting find with their classmates. First graders studying Japanese culture explore artifacts and photographs and interview a sushi chef. Fifth graders explore questions about equality, social justice, and equal rights as they study American history. They investigate their questions from a historical perspective, expressing their ideas in writing and art.

When kids are compelled by what they are learning and eager to know more, they develop what Tishman, Perkins, and Jay (1995) call a "strategic spirit." They define this as "a special kind of attitude encouraged in a culture of thinking, one that urges students to build and use thinking strategies in response to thinking and learning challenges" (1995, 3). Kids open their minds and hearts, wake up to possibilities, and exude an eagerness to ask questions and make sense of the world. When we foster a strategic spirit in our classrooms, the environment is rich with investigation, discussion, and collaboration.

We've said it before and we will say it again: Passion and wonder are contagious. We begin by modeling genuine curiosity about our world—what will happen with the simmering volcano in Indonesia?—and kids jump in with their comments and questions. We've never known a kid we can't hook onto something in the real world. A sense of possibility pervades the classroom and kids soon realize that the more we learn, the more we wonder. Questions abound and engagement soars, all day long. Even early in the morning, as we pick the kids up and walk them into the building, they burst with stories and queries. We don't just say great thinking and move on; we collaborate with them, showing how they can address questions with quick research and sharing how they can find out more. They know their thinking really does matter.

Curiosity in Action

Discovery center. Fourth and second graders, curious about fossils, team up to create an interactive "museum" in the classroom. Kids can't wait to get their hands on "real stuff." A discovery center has artifacts that relate to ongoing research and curricular inquiries. Kids identify and label specimens, create brochures, and set up activities to engage visitors.

This second grader creates her own discovery center at home, complete with a sign hanging from the tabletop that reads "Diskuvering Senter" (*sic*).

The discovery center fossil display includes field guides and observation sheets visitors can use for investigation.

Real-life experiences. A field trip, a talk from an expert, or simple immersion in a variety of related resources can inspire kids to wonder and ask questions.

Artifacts stoke first graders' curiosity. They jot new learning and questions about them.

Open-ended explorations immerse second graders in a new topic. Questions abound as kids figure out what bird built the nest, what materials were used to make it, and where it might have been located.

Reflecting on issues. Fifth graders ask authentic questions that emerge from their study of history. Kids' curiosity and questions can lead them from simple information to the problems or issues behind the facts. With curiosity in overdrive, they dig deep, responding with art and essays.

Who Had Equality?

Many of our founders like George Washington and Thomas Jefferson had many, many slaves, which hardly represents all men being equal. Actually, Thomas Jefferson had over 50 slaves while writing the Declaration of Independence. Why would they do this? Are they against equality or with it? . . .

There are so many questions about our past that we can't answer, but the ones that we can't answer are the important ones. So all the thoughts that are sitting in the back of our mind about who should have had equality, all of the questions you want to ask but are answerless, dare to ask them. Bring them out because you never know whether your thoughts and opinions could change the world! Look at our past mistakes and use them as inspiration to go forward.

In this excerpt from his essay "Who Had Equality?" a fifth grader explores the struggle for equality and equal rights throughout American history.

Kids' artwork expresses their take on issues such as equal rights.

Cornerstone 2. Workshop

We believe that workshop—a teaching approach based on an apprenticeship model—provides children with both the support and the freedom to become independent, thoughtful, agentive learners. The workshop environment fosters curiosity, comprehension, critical thinking, and collaboration because there are long blocks of time allotted for kids to read and write extensively as well as research content and talk about it. Teachers model their own process first and then empower kids to make decisions about their own learning.

Over time we have come to believe that kids should be in workshop all day long—not just during literacy time, but also when studying science and social studies. And even for math—although don't come to us for that one! Since we know and love reader's and writer's workshops for reading and writing, why not researcher's workshop for social studies and science? In researcher's workshop, kids read and investigate content-area topics. We share lessons to teach information, ideas, and issues in science, history, and social studies. When kids are engaged in a unit of study or inquiry, they respond by talking, drawing, making, writing, and researching further about what they learn. They actively use their knowledge as they share and teach others. Most of the inquiries that you see in this book take place in researcher's workshop.

Foundations of Workshop

Whether it's reader's, writer's, or researcher's, workshops in an inquiry-based classroom are organized around the following:

Access. Learning doesn't happen in a sterile environment. Kids need access to books and other resources, to materials that let them creatively respond, to content resources that support their curricular learning and spark their curiosity.

Choice. Beyond the constraints of mandated curriculum, kids need to be given choice—of readings, of forms of response, of topics to explore.

Response. Kids need ways to express and shape their thinking. Responding to what they are learning—by talking, drawing, building, performing—gives them a platform for their ideas.

Volume. We learn to read by reading, to write by writing, to research by researching. A lot.

Time. A successful and satisfying reading, writing, or research experience requires time—time to lose yourself in a book, to mess around with ways of expressing your ideas, to follow a concept or idea to the next step.

Ownership and engagement. Giving kids choice, access, and opportunities to respond; encouraging them to read, write, and research a lot; and providing the time to do it all creates engaged learners who take responsibility for their learning because they own it.

For further reading:

That Workshop Book
by S. Bennett

The Art of Teaching Writing
by L. Calkins

Building a Literate Classroom
by D. Graves

What's the Best That Can Happen?
by D. Miller

Workshop Structure

Since Donald Graves' early experiments with writer's workshop (Graves 1983), many permutations of writer's workshop (also called writing workshop) and reader's (or reading) workshop have evolved. However, the structure of the workshop has remained pretty much the same over time. Workshops typically last about an hour with the following elements in place:

- Explicit Instruction
- Conferring and Practice
- Sharing

Explicit instruction. Workshops often begin with a minilesson during which the teacher models her or his thinking for a few minutes so kids know what to do and what is expected of them. Not all lessons should be minilessons, however. The more complex the lesson, the more time needed to teach it—and the more time kids need to practice. So when teaching a concept or practice for the first time, we often engage kids in what we call *launch lessons*. These take longer than minilessons because as we model our thinking, we bring kids into the discussion, and we keep them up front working under our guidance. When we think they are ready to go, we send them off to practice collaboratively or on their own. Then on subsequent days, we reiterate what we taught in brief minilessons and release kids to practice what we taught. Many of the lessons that you will find in this book are launch lessons, which we follow up with minilessons.

Conferring as kids work. The bulk of time during the workshop is devoted to kids reading, writing, and researching as the teacher moves through the room conferring with and supporting them. Conferring allows teachers to target instruction to kids' individual learning needs. It is at the heart of workshop teaching.

Sharing. At the conclusion of the workshop, the teacher gathers the kids together to engage with each other and share their learning. Discussions highlight and reiterate the goals of the day's work.

The Gradual Release of Responsibility Lesson Structure for All Workshops

Engage	Teacher piques kids' interest and curiosity and ascertains and builds kids' background knowledge. Kids connect to their prior experiences and begin to build their knowledge.
Model	Teacher demonstrates a process, strategy, or technique, thinking aloud to help kids understand the process.
Guide	Still sitting up close as a group, kids try the process, strategy, or technique with the teacher prompting as necessary. The teacher can assess how well children understand the task and when they are ready for practice.
Practice	Kids practice collaboratively or independently as the teacher circulates and confers with individuals or small groups.
Share	Kids come together to summarize and share their learning, with discussion and dialogue that revisit the lesson goals and purposes.

Our workshops reflect a Gradual Release of Responsibility (GRR) framework. We gradually release responsibility for learning to the student. GRR is the scaffold upon which our workshops are built.

Workshop in Action

Don Graves says, "Teach the reader, not the reading; the writer, not the writing." And we would add, the same goes for research. Learning workshop routines builds kids' independence whether it's reading, writing, or research.

Explicit instruction. Fourth graders participate in an interactive read-aloud, which encourages discussion and debate. These longer launch lessons are opportunities for important conversations.

Independent and collaborative practice. Time for kids to wade in and tackle a text, a task, or a problem—whether on their own or with a partner or partners—is the key to learning. As teachers, our role during practice is to confer, tailoring instruction to individual needs and interests.

During practice, a second grader shares with and gets advice from a friend.

Kindergarten teacher Kristen Elder-Rubino confers with a student during researcher's workshop.

Second graders choose from options during independent practice.

Take thinking public by sharing. In addition to building a sense of community and validating kids' work, consistent sharing sessions augment learning. Kids not only learn a lot from one another but also get ideas they can try out themselves.

One second grader shares his writing. Kids run the share themselves, chiming in with questions, comments, or connections.

Informal small-group and partner shares happen all day and every day.

Cornerstone 3. Content

"*Teachers hold the energy and vision for the inquiry.*"

—Karen Halverson

For further reading:

Short Nonfiction for Teaching American History series by S. Harvey and A. Goudvis

To Look Closely: Science and Literacy in the Natural World by L. Rubin

Making Sense of History by M. Zarnowski

www.scienceandliteracy.org

In recent years, science, history, and other content areas have been relegated to the back burner in too many classrooms. The tremendous emphasis on testing and accountability has resulted in a laserlike focus on literacy, knocking other subjects right off the curricular radar screen. We believe it's time to correct these curricular imbalances—to bring back science, history, and other content topics with a vengeance. How to do this? Ta-da! Through researcher's workshop!

When we walk into a workshop classroom, we don't know if it's reader's, writer's, or researcher's workshop until we look at the texts and the topics kids are reading and writing about. If all of the books and articles are on extreme weather, it's a pretty good bet you have entered the researcher's workshop. Kids still have ample choice in text and inquiries but they are focused on content from the curriculum. Researcher's workshop is where we teach science, history, literature, and social studies.

Curricular inquiries are the bread and butter of researcher's workshop. We strongly believe that we need to devote as much time to science and social studies as we do to other subject areas. Since time is always an obstacle, we suggest that we spend a few weeks in researcher's workshop on a social studies topic and then the next several weeks on science. Some of these topics lend themselves to integration. Others not so much.

Most of the inquiries that happen during researcher's workshop (at least in this resource) are curriculum based. We're with Jerome Bruner (2009), who long ago argued that almost any curricular topic can be designed and shaped in a way that engages and challenges kids of varying ages (not to mention us teachers). But we relish and honor kids' interests and passions, so we make time during or after a curricular inquiry for kids to go off and investigate their interests and questions.

As we introduce kids to the inquiry process, teachers play an essential role in maintaining the big picture of where the inquiry is going and what we want to accomplish. We see the possibilities and potential of the inquiry and have a clear sense of topics and issues that will engage and motivate kids. The whole process is carefully scaffolded to teach kids to become researchers—with important ideas and concepts front and center.

Content in Action

Inquiry can drive learning in any content area. For example, author studies in reading, mentor text analyses in writing, and primary source research in history and social studies all bear the hallmarks of an inquiry approach. And, of course, the scientific method is the embodiment of inquiry.

Second-Grade Scientists

Second-grade district science standards focus on teaching kids to think and study as scientists do. Heisey and Kucan (2011) suggest that kids learn about scientific thinking by reading about scientists and their exciting discoveries. After studying paleontology with dinosaur finder Mary Anning and snow crystals with Snowflake Bentley, kids are ready to become ornithologists. With John James Audubon as a mentor, they observe and research local birds, set up bird feeders to watch bird behavior, and create field guides to share with their families.

Thinking and learning like scientists. Kids are immersed in science experiences including close observation, sketching and writing about what they are learning, studying just like practicing scientists do. To provide these in-depth experiences, we connect kids with experts and specialists, online resources, and real-life observations.

Specimens and artifacts from the local university allow kids to explore models of extinct animals and stone tools as part of a unit on paleontology and fossils. They create their own museum for visitors to the classroom.

Kids observe birds close up, with bird feeders hung right outside the classroom window. Observation fuels their study as they emulate scientists like John James Audubon.

Reading, writing, and thinking in social studies and history. For us history buffs, history is all about "enduring human dramas and dilemmas, fascinating mysteries, and an amazing cast of historical characters involved in events that exemplify the best and worst of human experiences" (Bain 2007). But too often kids experience social studies and history as a dull slog through a mountain of facts in the textbook.

Fourth- and Fifth-Grade Historians

In this inquiry-based classroom, the focus is on understanding multiple perspectives, as students study Westward Expansion, the American Revolution, and so on. Kids delve into primary sources, videos, articles and blogs, TED talks, artistic images and photographs, websites, and both historical and realistic fiction, all of which contribute to a more accurate picture of what happened in history as well as what's going on in the world right now.

Karen's lesson books function as notebooks for researcher's workshop.

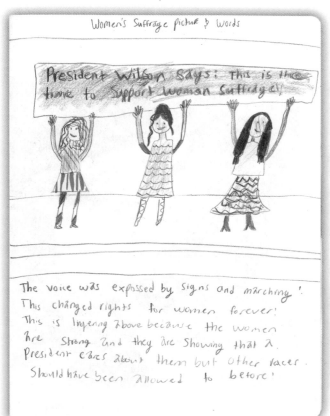

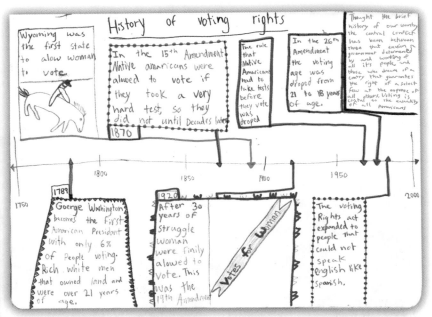

Lesson books hold intermediate kids' written responses, artistic representations, poetry, and everything else about class content topics. Like researcher's notebooks, they provide an ongoing record of evolving thinking and learning over time.

Cornerstone 4. Comprehension

You can't teach content without teaching kids how to think about it. Comprehension is at the core of our teaching. We teach comprehension across the day and throughout the year to foster understanding and engagement, and to build knowledge. Cervetti, Jaynes, and Hiebert (2009) suggest that knowledge building is the new frontier in literacy instruction, because "reading instruction is more potent when it builds and then capitalizes upon the development of content knowledge." Strategies are tools kids use to make meaning when they read, hear, and view. Comprehension instruction deepens learning in different disciplines, in science, social studies, language arts, and so forth. Throughout the day in all workshops, kids use thinking strategies such as these to analyze, debate, discuss, respond, generate new knowledge, and take action.

For further reading:

Strategies That Work, 3rd edition, by S. Harvey and A. Goudvis

The Comprehension Toolkit series by S. Harvey and A. Goudvis

Reading with Meaning, 2nd edition, by D. Miller

- **Monitor understanding** Kids learn to recognize when information makes sense, when it doesn't, and adjust to make meaning. Kids learn to listen to their inner voice as they read.

- **Activate, access, and connect to background knowledge** Kids connect to what they already know and learn to recognize when new knowledge changes their thinking. As P. David Pearson says, "Today's new knowledge is tomorrow's background knowledge" (2006). It's the foundation that allows kids to gain insight and understanding, and even take action, through reading and learning.

- **Ask authentic questions** Curiosity is at the heart of teaching and learning. Questioning is the strategy that propels readers forward. Kids' questions launch their inquiries. Honoring kids' thinking and questions creates a classroom rich with possibilities and opportunities for learning.

- **Infer and visualize** Kids read between the lines, discern themes and important ideas, and deepen understanding; visualizing brings written words to life. Inferring is the bedrock of comprehension—it's what adds richness and depth to our understanding as we encounter texts, images, videos, and many other resources.

- **Determine importance** Kids sort and sift information to come up with the most important ideas. Barraged with information 24-7, it's essential for kids to shape what they are learning into their own thoughts.

- **Summarize and synthesize information and ideas** Kids process and distill information to understand it and make it their own. They add to their store of knowledge, merging new information with what they already know. We may come to understand a new perspective, a new line of thinking, and come up with original ideas based on what we read, listen to, and view.

A Comprehension Continuum

Acquiring and actively using knowledge provides a strong foundation for fostering understanding. The Comprehension Continuum (Harvey and Daniels 2015) illustrates a whole spectrum of comprehension possibilities, from an emphasis on literal questions and retellings to strategic thinking that encourages

Comprehension Continuum

Answer Literal Questions	Retell	Merge Thinking with Content	Acquire Knowledge	Actively Use Knowledge
Answering literal questions shows that learners can skim and scan for answers, pick one out that matches the question, and have short-term recall. *Only demonstrates surface understandings.*	Retelling shows that learners can organize thoughts sequentially and put them into their own words. Shows short-term recall of events in a narrative and bits of information in nonfiction. *Does not, in and of itself, demonstrate understanding.*	Real understanding takes root when learners merge their thinking with the content by connecting, inferring, visualizing, questioning, determining importance, synthesizing, and reacting to information. *Understanding begins here.*	Once learners have merged their thinking with the content, they can begin to acquire knowledge and insight. They can learn, understand, and remember. *Shows more learning and robust understanding.*	With new insights and understandings, learners can actively use knowledge and apply what they have learned to other experiences and situations. They expand their understanding and may even take action. *Understanding used for problem-solving and acting.*
Teacher Language	**Teacher Language**	**Teacher Language**	**Teacher Language**	**Teacher Language**
What is _____? Where did _____? Who was _____? How did _____? How many _____?	Tell me what happened. What was the story about? Retell what you read. What comes first, second, third? When did _____?	What do you think? What did you learn? What does this remind you of? What do you wonder? What do you visualize? What do you infer? What is this mostly about? What makes you say/think that? How did you come up with that? What, if anything, confuses you?	What did you learn that you think is important to remember? Why does it matter? What do you think the author most wants you to get out of this? What evidence can you cite to make your claim? What do you think are some big ideas here? What difference does it make? How would you evaluate this information?	What do you want to do about this? Why do you want to take action? How might you take action? Is there a way you can get involved? How do you think you can help? How would you convince others of your point of view? What is your plan? How might you engage the help of others?

(Adapted from Harvey and Daniels 2015)

actively using knowledge in a myriad of ways. The continuum is not sequential in nature but rather a continuum of sophistication, moving from literal understanding to the active use of knowledge. It illustrates how learners comprehend and reflects the language teachers use to scaffold kids' thinking depending on different purposes for reading and responding.

■ From Strategic Reading to Critical and Creative Thinking

Strategic reading and thinking, as described in the middle column of the continuum, are a bridge to active and engaged learning on the right side of the continuum (Durham 2009, personal communication). Strategic reading refers to thinking about reading (and also viewing and listening) in ways that enhance learning and understanding.

Answer Literal Questions *and* Retells

The left side of the continuum, answering literal questions, is too often where comprehension begins and ends—kids experience end-of-the-chapter questions, test-prep exercises, and recitation sessions where the teacher asks questions and kids respond. Retelling, the next point on the continuum, involves recounting events in a narrative or recalling factual information. Although literal understanding of information and an ability to restate facts or events in a story is important, comprehension is much more than "just the facts."

Merge Thinking with Content

Authentic comprehension and understanding happen when kids use strategies such as monitoring, asking questions, inferring, and determining what's important to merge their thinking with content. Kids activate what they already know and merge it with new information, turning that information into knowledge (Harvey and Goudvis 2017). As kids inquire and investigate with content topics, opportunities for genuine learning happen.

Acquire Knowledge *and* Actively Use Knowledge

Learning, understanding, and remembering are active, intentional processes. It goes without saying that kids construct their own knowledge. We can't do it for them. When they do this, they often take their learning in original and unforeseen directions and transfer their knowledge to new situations and topics. Kids develop their own take on an issue or problem. Actively using knowledge engages us in discovery and leads us to imagine possibilities. It enables us to see different sides of an issue and develop empathy and compassion that lead to action based on what we have learned and believe. Kids begin to take their knowledge public, teach others, and put it to use in the world.

Critical and creative thinking. When kids think critically, they are analytical and reflective, and they entertain a variety of different perspectives. Kids can't swallow hook, line, and sinker everything they read, hear, or view. In a 24-7 info-culture bursting with "fake news" and "alternative facts," not to mention nonstop interactions on social media, it's more important than ever for kids to read, view, and listen with a critical eye and a skeptical stance. And they need to engage in meaningful dialogue—with their peers, parents, teachers, and, eventually, the big, wide world out there.

Creative thinking (as defined by Sternberg and Williams 1996, quoted in Vinton 2018) happens when kids "imagine, explore, synthesize, connect, discover, invent, and adapt." To this list, we'd add open-ended, expansive, out-of-the-box thinking. Kids are encouraged to imagine and invent ways to express themselves through art, music, poetry, and drama. Our mantra is: What we envision, we can create.

Both critical and creative thinking are essential twenty-first-century skills. According to Johnston (2004), kids who have a sense of agency have confidence in their own abilities to make things happen. Whether it's sharing insights about the themes in a picture book, or composing and performing in a poetry slam presentation, agency matters.

We teachers are the critical and creative thinkers-in-chief, building the classroom culture so these kinds of thinking flourish. As kids create artistic responses, teachers are right there, drawing and sketching along with them. When kids decide to take a stand on an issue, they learn how to persuade others or advocate by taking action. What's most important is that we demonstrate taking risks and stretching out of our comfort zones—and then the kids take it from there.

To foster critical and creative thinking, we model and share practices that encourage kids to

- reread, rethink, and reflect
- adopt a skeptical stance
- look beneath and beyond the information given to analyze, interpret, and gain insight
- ask probing questions about information, ideas, evidence, and so forth
- imagine the world from multiple perspectives and develop empathy
- suspend judgment and give credence to varied opinions, interpretations, and ideas
- synthesize information and ideas across disciplines
- create their own take on information and issues, imagine possibilities, and formulate original interpretations
- integrate thinking to see all facets of a problem
- create artistic, musical, poetic, and dramatic expressions of learning and understanding
- value out-of-the-box thinking and learning, honor imagination and invention
- engage in open-ended conversation that builds on others' ideas and thoughts
- develop world awareness: be a global citizen aware of our impact on the environment and society both close to home and beyond.

Comprehension in Action

Kids showcase their understanding every time they make a comment, ask a question, participate in a discussion, or create an artistic response to what they are learning.

Simulating experiences and reflecting on them. Third graders learn about what it's like to be a refugee in a simulated refugee camp set up by Doctors Without Borders. The organization set up tents, rafts, and exhibits for visitors to experience from the inside out. Experiencing a historic or current event and then talking and writing about that experience enhances comprehension and understanding.

This third grader holds pictures of what she chose to take with her on her journey as a "refugee"— a cell phone, water, shoes. It's not easy for kids to understand people whose lives are vastly different from their own. To more fully comprehend this experience, she wrote a reflection: "If you had to flee so fast you might not be able to grab anything and if you did, you would have to choose quickly. You may not be able to grab the things you love the most."

Another reflection: "My favorite station was the second station, where we were fleeing all together on a raft, and the waves were really big. I learned that the men would sit on the outside and all the women and children in the middle and it was dangerous. I learned how scary and dangerous being a refugee is."

Reflecting on new learning to better comprehend it. Carefully selected picture books encourage kids to explore sophisticated and abstract ideas and themes with interactive read-alouds. Kids spend several weeks listening to a variety of books about kindness, fairness, prejudice, and doing the right thing, so their understanding of these significant themes deepens over time.

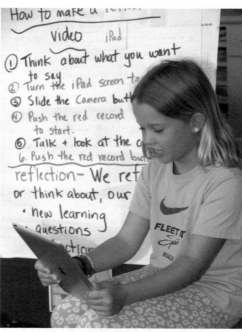

This second grader synthesizes her new learning with a reflection video, following the directions on the chart.

First graders talk about big ideas during an interactive read-aloud to more fully understand the story. After reading, they write and draw their thinking about important ideas, such as friendship.

Building knowledge. During researcher's workshop, kids demonstrate their growing understanding in many different ways—through posters, brochures, digital stories, and so on. Their creations in art and writing demonstrate their new knowledge.

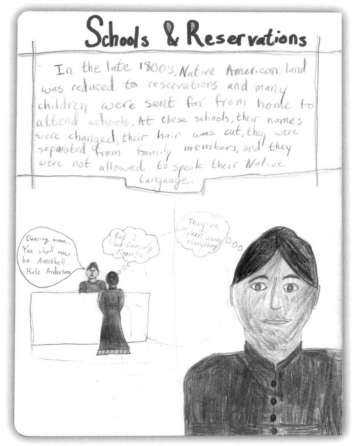

Lesson books (or researcher's notebooks) hold kids' artistic and written understandings. This cover and page from two lesson books illustrate fourth graders' creative and critical thinking about encounters between Native Americans and settlers in American history.

Second graders create digital reports on weather events, such as tornadoes.

Cornerstone 5. Collaboration

Kids build relationships with each other and all adults in the environment to create a community of learners. We begin by thinking about the kinds of interactions and communication that we encourage every day in our classrooms. What matters is that kids feel welcome and are comfortable taking risks and expressing their thoughts. Mutual respect and regard for each and every person in the room is paramount. A vibrant, empathetic classroom community is far more likely when kids feel ownership of what happens every day. And remember, to have a collaborative classroom we need a collaborative staff.

Above all we focus on relationships, helping kids getting to know one another. We encourage them to take responsibility for participating in and contributing to life in the classroom, beginning on the first day of school. We also focus on the physical space and plan and create an environment that supports collaborative inquiry.

A collaborative community requires communication. As teachers we know a lot about getting kids to talk in the classroom, and we encourage far more kid talk than teacher talk. Interaction through talk is the most underrepresented form of communication in schools. Large-scale studies of intermediate grades found that "students spend only 7% of the school day in small groups where they collaborate on tasks . . . (so that) kids became much more active and involved in their learning" (Pianta et al. 2007). Studies like these suggest kids spend way too much time in passive rather than active learning.

Kids acquire and use knowledge by thinking and talking about it. To paraphrase James Britton, who said, "literacy floats on a sea of talk," we believe it's also true that "*understanding* floats on a sea of talk." Individual time for reading, writing, and researching is crucial, but purposeful talk and conversation is the foundation of our teaching and kids' learning. To foster this, we create intentional groups where kids interact and in which they have a common purpose.

■ Types of Classroom Talk

We outline these various types of classroom talk to emphasize that collaboration happens when teachers and kids co-construct meaning. The last thing we want to do is fire questions at kids in the Initiation, Response, Evaluation (Mehan 1979) mode described here. When teachers do all the talking, student curiosity, ownership, and engagement shut down. When teachers talk too much, inquiry suffers.

We have long advocated that kids adopt and adapt our teaching language as their learning language. If we want kids to listen to each other, build on each other's thinking, engage in respectful conversations, and encourage each other in collaborative research, we need to create the conditions for this to happen.

For further reading:

Comprehension and Collaboration, 2nd edition, by S. Harvey and H. Daniels

Choice Words and *Opening Minds* by P. Johnston

Engaging Children by E. Keene

Comprehension Through Conversation by M. Nichols

Types of Classroom Talk

Type of Talk	What Is It?	Good for Discussion?
Talk That Limits Discussion and Conversation		
Initiation, Response, Evaluation (Mehan 1979) *Purpose:* Teacher assesses learned facts from reading or lecture.	Teacher asks question with known answer. Student responds. Teacher praises or moves on to next student. T: Does the Nile River flow through Egypt? S: Yes. T: Excellent.	No. IRE promotes what Ritchhart names a "ping-pong dialogue": a back-and-forth between teacher and students.
Display Question (Cazden 2001) *Purpose:* Teacher and students review and check facts.	Teacher asks a question with a known answer. Student responds. T: What is the largest city in Colorado? S: Denver.	No. Conversation is between one student and the teacher.
Talk That Supports Engagement and Inquiry		
Exploratory Talk (Cazden 2001) *Purpose:* Students develop ideas, collaborate, and recognize that talking and conversation brings better understanding.	Students explore ideas by talking about them. S1: I wonder if this fossil is an insect . . . or what is it? S2: It looks like it has a shell, but it could also be like a sea creature with a shell. S3: Yeah, I think it's called a trilobite, but let's check the field guide. S1: So is a trilobite a kind of insect?	Yes. Students take over and connect their thinking to the idea presented.
Instructional Conversation (Saunders and Goldenberg 2007) *Purpose:* Conversation to explore ideas together as a group.	Classroom talk that is give-and-take. Students take turns chiming in, becoming alert to when someone is done. S1: Why did the pioneers think they could build their homes on Native American lands? T: Interesting question. What do you all think about this? S2: Pioneers had the idea of manifest destiny—that the country was theirs and they should take it over. S3: But that doesn't make it right. After all, the Native Americans were there first. T: As you all suggest, there are many reasons for the conflicts between Native Americans and settlers. We'll be exploring these different perspectives.	Yes. Students take over and talk, taking turns, listening, and responding to others' thinking. And the listener has the most important job, taking notes on questions, confusions, and new learning.
Conversational Uptakes (Stipek 2002) *Purpose:* Teacher scaffolds language to build from students' approximations.	Teacher interjects comments to keep students' conversation going. S1: Bats hunt at night. S2: That means they are . . . what's the word? T: Nocturnal. Like raccoons. They hunt at night. S1: We sleep at night.	Yes. Conversational uptakes happen during give-and-take conversations. They promote talk for students with a range of language experience.

(Mohr and Mohr 2007)

Conversation protocols. We foster collaboration through conversation. We teach specific ways to work productively, share respectfully, and engage with everyone in the classroom (and beyond). We often post language frames in a prominent place to remind kids of language they use as they work together.

Discussion is one of the primary ways we model collaborative and idea-centered conversations. It is a way to explore issues and problems, to imagine possibilities, and to think outside the box. Building kids' confidence in expressing themselves is integral to their participation in a collaborative community of learners. Sometimes kids' spontaneous conversation is productive. Sometimes it's not. We use open-ended discussion prompts repeatedly to give kids a sense

Joining a Group

Student: May I join your group?

Group: Sure, here's what we are doing.

Student: What should I do to help?

Group: Would you mind _____?

How about if you _____?

We really need help with _____.

Sharing Respectfully

Teacher: Roberto, would you like to share what you learned/think/wonder/feel?

Student 1: Yes, thank you. (*Student shares. Then invites another.*)

Student 1: Annaliese, would you like to share what you learned/think/wonder/feel?

Student 2: Yes, thank you.

Disagreeing Agreeably

We want kids to feel comfortable disagreeing with peers and adults, but we want them to do it respectfully, and we need to give them the tools to do so. We teach them language frames like these:

I beg to differ _____.

That's interesting, I have another idea _____.

I heard what _____ said, but I see it a little differently.

I used to think that, but now I think _____.

Turning and Talking

What We Do	What We Say
Turn our heads to look at each other.	Would you like to go first?
Move your body to sit close to your partner.	Sure, I'll start. I think _____. What do you think?
Listen! That's the most important job.	This makes me think _____. Tell me more _____.
Take turns talking and sharing.	That's interesting _____.

Partner Reading

What We Do	What We Say
Sit next to each other with the same book.	Would you like to read? Yes, thank you.
Decide who will read each part.	I'll read a page. You read a page.
Take turns reading and talking.	I was thinking about this picture. Do you have any connections? What are you wondering? Why? What do you think about this part? I'd like to stop and talk about this.

of agency, so they get the message that their thinking matters and learn ways to share their thinking and ideas with others. We

- encourage kids to internalize and use them independently in conversations and interactions.
- help kids understand anything they hear, see, or read more completely by prompting them to work out the meaning.

Discussion prompts. Some question prompts we've adapted from Peter Johnston's books *Choice Words* (2004) and *Opening Minds* (2011) follow. Keep in mind that these are not questions with an intended answer, but rather questions to encourage discussion and conversation.

"We learn from the company we keep."
—Frank Smith

Discussion Prompts		
Listening	**Viewing**	**Reading**
What do the words make you think about?	What do you notice/observe?	What in the text makes you say that?
What did you hear?	What does the image remind you of?	How do you know?
What does it remind you of?	What do you wonder?	What makes you think that? Tell me more about your thinking.
What did you hear that makes you think that?	What do the graphics/features make you think about?	Where is there evidence for your thinking?
What do you want to hear more about?	What do you infer from the photo/image/graphic?	Where in the text did you get that idea? Who has another idea? Who might respectfully disagree?
What did you hear that is evidence for that idea?	Where is the evidence for that idea?	How might you explain the different interpretations?
Do you agree or disagree? Why or why not?	What in the image makes you say or think that?	What kind of evidence does the author use?
		What do you think? Explain whether you disagree or agree— say some more.

(Adapted from Johnston 2004, 2011)

Collaboration in Action

Community building happens in many ways: through a variety of shared experiences and by repeatedly welcoming kids' input into classroom life.

Collaborating on space. Second graders collaborated to designate a museum exhibit area in the classroom.

Other students visit the classroom, sitting in the museum display area to learn about penguins and their egg-laying behavior.

Message board. Second graders communicate through letters, notes, and even photos on a message board. Comments, requests, suggestions, and questions on this interactive board build ownership and collaboration.

Socratic seminars. Socratic seminars are student-led conversations that begin with a question or an issue to be discussed. Fourth graders learn to run the discussion themselves.

Kids cite evidence from text and images to support their positions and responses.

Collaborative inquiry. Collective action is a powerful way for kids to celebrate the work they have done as a community, express their opinions, and take a stand.

Fifth graders engage in a "get out the vote" demonstration on a university campus, right before election day.

Cornerstone 6. Classroom Environment

Before school even begins, we ask ourselves: How can we arrange our teaching space to ensure the kind of dynamic, interactive, engaged learning we envision? We set up a welcoming space for kids as they walk in the door on day one, knowing we will adapt it to kids' needs and interests and leaving room for them to make the environment their own.

Our three priorities for making sure our classrooms support discovery and inquiry are to:

- create purposeful work spaces
- gather and organize tools and resources
- design ways to make thinking and learning visible.

Inquiry-based learning is not about a culminating project to a unit, but rather about living in a way that kids' questions matter and about setting up classrooms that foster curiosity all day and every day.

■ Purposeful Work Spaces

There's a productive hum as kids spread out around the room during work time. One group observes and sketches a giant cockroach in a terrarium, learning that they have been around for millions of years. Several kids illustrate poems they've written about a recent solar eclipse, referring to images and vocabulary on a content word wall. Yet another pair surveys everyone in the class, finding out kids' opinions and ideas for new playground equipment.

Workspaces include:

- nooks and seating options that are responsive to kids' personal preferences
- varied spaces for formal, large-group lessons and small-group research
- cozy nooks for quiet study or a place for a book group
- areas designed by kids.

We are great fans of something colloquially known as "classroom makeovers"—carving out time in the few days before school starts when teachers are back at work to collaborate as a group on room setup. As a small group of willing souls moves from one room to another, each person shares his or her goals and challenges with respect to the environment. The group listens. Then we brainstorm possibilities and together come up with ideas for organizing the space. With collaboration and muscle power, voilà! What we envision becomes reality. And then it's on to the next classroom.

For further reading:

Ladybugs, Tornadoes, and Swirling Galaxies: English Language Learners Discover Their World Through Inquiry by B. Buhrow and A. Garcia

The whole-group area is center stage. Engagement soars when students have plenty of room to share projects, create dramatizations, and even perform.

A large rug area has a lot of flexibility and comfortable spaces to accommodate small groups during work time, such as this fourth-grade book club.

Second graders weigh in with how classroom space is used. They requested a place to write to their pen pals on postcards, so the nook is stocked with materials for corresponding.

Remember to include comfortable spaces for quiet concentration in the midst of a busy day.

Creative use of space

A former storage area in the hallway morphs into a studio space with many possibilities. Flexible seating, wall space, laptops, and places to display materials and resources provide everything kids need for exploration and study. Whiteboards reflect each step in the research process: Immerse, Investigate, Coalesce, and Take Public. As inquiries unfold, kids fill the space and walls with their questions, new learning, and projects.

■ Accessible Tools and Resources

Reading, writing, and research are what we do. Appealing and accessible print and digital resources to read and view as well as materials for writing and creating give kids the tools they need when they need them. Kids assume the responsibility for keeping the room in order. They are mindful of conserving resources.

Kids sort and organize books into categories. They explain the system to the rest of the class so that everyone can help with upkeep.

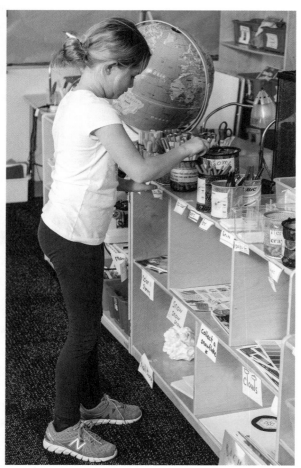

Artistic expression is honored and valued, so materials are plentiful and enticing.

■ Making Thinking Visible

Halls and walls teach. Visual displays of co-constructed anchor charts illustrate and guide teaching and learning over time. Displays of kids' writing and art feature a highly visible record of kids' finished projects and in-progress thinking. When students consistently share their questions and interests, they come to know each other as learners. Collaboration becomes a way of life.

We begin the year with blank walls and bulletin boards. Why decorate with stuff from the teacher store when very soon the halls and walls will be filled with more interesting examples of kids' learning and our teaching?

Throughout this book, kids make their thinking visible by annotating both information and thinking. Post-its, two- and three-column think sheets, and large charts are opportunities for kids to draw and write their way into under-standing.

Anchor charts. Anchor charts are essential tools for teaching in ways that make kids' thinking and learning visible and concrete. They provide an ongoing record of instruction as it unfolds each day. Charts of all kinds cover walls, easels, any place kids can see and use them. When space is a challenge, we change them up often, making sure they are relevant and useful.

Here's a short list of options for co-constructing anchor charts:

- Include the language of instruction so kids begin to internalize it. Our teaching language becomes the kids' learning language.
- Honor kids' work and thinking by adding their responses to the charts. Their Post-its, responses, and ideas spark conversation and discussion.
- Send the message that we are a community of teachers and learners— our conversations and ideas are worth recording and "making visible" so we can revisit and discuss these over time.
- Keep the language clear. Charts are referred to by kids who rely on them for guiding what they do and how they talk, especially language for comprehension and thinking strategies and procedures (how to choose a book to read, how to write a picture book; steps for the research process).
- Collaborate with students. Charts are not only co-constructed (teachers and kids) but also kid-driven/-constructed. When kids create their own teaching/learning/response charts, they are assuming ownership and responsibility. Kids might list their burning questions, their discoveries, their new learning—and other kids respond.
- Provide parents and visitors to the classroom a clear, coherent idea of what we are thinking and learning and send the message that this is what matters.
- Spotlight kids' original ideas and creative expression.

Second graders illustrate procedural charts as handy references to guide them during independent reading.

Content charts reflect new learning in an inquiry as well as responses to focus questions.

Kids' work. Gone are the days of twenty-eight nearly identical state reports posted on the bulletin board. Showcasing kids' work on walls and in hallways—both finished and in-progress—sends the message that this is their classroom and they are sharing what happens there. But it's not just about a display—it's for teaching and learning, both inside and outside of the classroom. When kids' work is visible and public, this

- provides authentic opportunities for kids to teach and learn from each other
- shows the development and trajectory of kids' progress and understanding over time
- inspires responses, reactions, and conversations among classmates, with other kids in the school, with parents and other visitors
- celebrates the intensive thinking and hard work that go into kids' efforts to take their learning public and make it attractive and engaging for readers and viewers.

Not everything we put up needs to be in "final" form. We use draft stamps or place "work in progress" signs on kids' work when they share drafts and other ongoing work. What better way to get thoughtful feedback and guidance for adding to one's work and thinking?

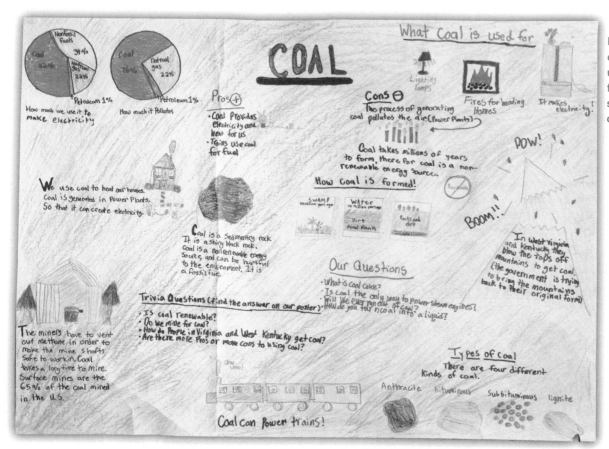

Fourth graders create an infographic using a variety of features and text to share information on complex topics.

Walls are interactive, so kids respond on Post-its right on displayed work. Learning is a collaborative venture and walls are a great place to try out ideas and share in-progress thinking.

Visitors, parents, kids, and teachers take part in a collaborative conversation about the picture book *Separate Is Never Equal*, by Duncan Tonatiuh.

We post student work in the hallway for the community to read and learn from. The book *Separate Is Never Equal* is a story about school desegregation in California in the 1960s. Parents, teachers, and visitors respond with their comments on Post-its.

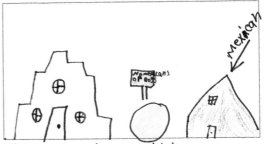

We read <u>Separate is Never Equal.</u>

This story makes me think......

This story made me think that Sylvia's parents worked very hard to make her be able to go the school.

We read <u>Separate is Never Equal.</u>

This story makes me think......

That if you fight for something that you don't think is right, you almost always will get something good out of it. I also feel like when you express your voice, people who are scared to stand up for themselves will be grateful for you.

These are very thoughtful responses about people standing up for their rights.
Ms. T

We read <u>Separate is Never Equal.</u>

This story makes me think......

about other people not only mexicans should have a voice. Also that people try their best to take action. Also that some people are scared for deportation and immigrants can not even go to stores because they think that the police I.C.E will get them.

You all are discussing such important issues—which are happening right now!
Mia's dad

Researcher's Workshop

"Research is formalized curiosity. It is poking and prying with a purpose."

—Zora Neale Hurston

During researcher's workshop, kids investigate in science, history, and other content subjects every day. They read, write, draw, and create, propelled by the momentum of their curiosity. This chapter on researcher's workshop is the heart of this book. To avoid the chaos that sometimes overwhelms the inquiry process, we suggest a gradual-release approach to keep teachers sane and kids on track. We have designed a scaffolded process to support teachers and kids as they experiment with and delve deeper into inquiry.

So it's really gradual release for inquiry. To illustrate our gradual-release approach, we share how the research process plays out in Brad Buhrow's second-grade classroom, beginning with launching, moving to guiding, and eventually supporting independent inquiries. For each of the three inquiries shared here, we have created generic frameworks with practices you can adopt and adapt to your own curricular topics.

Front and center in this chapter are the core practices and lessons we use to teach the research process. Additional reading and writing practices that we introduce in reader's, writer's, and researcher's workshops are described in the following chapter "Reading and Writing in Support of Inquiry."

The Gradual Release of Inquiry-Based Learning

We have found that to effectively teach the inquiry process, we need to follow the Gradual Release of Responsibility approach. Over a number of years of engaging kids in inquiry-based learning, we have discovered that the most effective way to lead them through a year of inquiry and develop proficient researchers is to make a distinction between launching, guiding, and independent inquiry. We know inquiry-based teaching often seems challenging. We've had our share of flops when we've turned kids loose to "do research" without adequately preparing them. So it occurred to us that breaking the research process down makes a lot of sense. Brad's launching, guiding, and independent inquiry trajectory provides kids with the scaffolded approach that builds independence over time.

This chapter describes what happens as teachers and kids engage in each of these inquiries.

Launching Inquiry

When we first engage in inquiry learning, there is a lot for kids to learn how to do. We teachers demonstrate the entire process as we go through the inquiry as a class. We flood the room with resources. We model how we ask questions. We come up with a researchable question and as a group investigate it together. We show kids ways to synthesize learning and take it public. But the goal is to teach kids the process so they begin to internalize it and become increasingly able to research on their own.

Guiding Inquiry

After kids have become familiar with the research process through one or more launching experiences, we plan for ways to give them more independence in pursuing investigations and sharing their learning. We design an inquiry that builds in more time for kids to take responsibility for asking questions, narrowing them down, addressing their questions through investigation, and sharing their learning in a variety of ways. But we continue to model the research process to reinforce it and guide kids as necessary.

Children differ and access learning strategies at different paces. So we remember to attend to their individual differences and desires.

Supporting Independent Inquiry

Kids will access the inquiry process in different ways and at different paces. Some may be ready to go after a single launch. Others need more time and guidance. But what we have learned is that kids are more successful at independent inquiry if they have a common experience with it first and have had some time to practice. In the independent inquiry process, kids do the majority of the work with teachers weighing in as needed to support them.

A caveat: If you are an intermediate teacher in a school that has featured an inquiry approach to content learning for a number of years, it is likely that with a bit of review, you can launch your first inquiry as a guided inquiry and move to independent inquiries soon thereafter. Where we land on this inquiry continuum has everything to do with how much time we have spent teaching in this way and how much experience our kids have with inquiry-based learning.

Over the course of the school year, kids are engaged in authentic, experiential, thoughtful inquiries so that they build an abiding interest in finding things out. These efforts result in diverse, child-authored and -illustrated projects, such as posters, slide decks, letters to the editor or powers that be, digital books, poems, videos, and so on. Note that the sample projects included here are simply suggestions. The idea is to give kids so much to think about that they come up with original (and often far more interesting!) ways to share all their new learning. We want classrooms brimming with kids who are enthusiastic, independent learners, so we make sure kids have the time, materials, and reading/thinking strategies that allow them to explore their own learning.

In this chapter, you'll find:

- ideas for designing inquiries
- core practices and lessons for researcher's workshop
- generic frameworks so you can plan inquiries with your curricular topics
- examples of launching, guiding, and supporting independent inquiries and how practices play out across the inquiry framework (Immerse, Investigate, Coalesce, Take Public).

Designing Inquiries

As we design inquiries, we teachers have had to rethink our approach to content and curricular topics. We consider the content and strategies kids need to learn and plan ways for kids to become immersed in a topic through a variety of entry points, exploring intriguing resources or engaging in real-life experiences. We tease out compelling questions that cross disciplines and subject areas. We scout out real-world connections through video, web resources, interviews, and field trips that make topics relevant and easy to connect to. Rethinking a curricular topic in light of our inquiry framework requires us to begin with enduring understandings and essential questions and then relish the search for materials, resources, and lessons that will excite and engage kids and bring the topic to life. But kids are our coconspirators in all this—we take seriously their interests and ideas for ways to enhance and expand on the inquiry, which often results in serendipitous and meaningful discoveries.

■ Enduring Understandings and Essential Questions

We begin with enduring understandings and essential questions, for they will define everything we do along the inquiry journey. We return to these again and again, for clarity, focus, and purpose, as we plan, teach, and learn. These encapsulate the essential learnings we want students to grapple with, ponder, apply to their lives, and take into the world.

Enduring Understandings

> "Enduring understandings are statements that summarize important ideas and core processes that are central to a discipline and have lasting value beyond the classroom. They synthesize what students should understand—not just know—as a result of studying a particular content area, and they articulate what students should revisit over the course of their lifetimes in relationship to the content area."
>
> —Jay McTighe and Grant Wiggins, *Understanding by Design*

Enduring understandings can emerge from a variety of sources. One place to start is with core standards. Reading through core standard documents, we look for relationships between the big ideas and grade-level concepts. Then we ask ourselves, "How can we craft a statement that summarizes and connects these ideas in a universal and transferable way?"

Another place from which to extract enduring understandings lies within the texts and materials we use to create an inquiry. Reading through trade books, picture books, professional books, and online articles, we look for themes, ideas, and concepts that come up again and again, and we consider how they all connect. We ask ourselves, "What are the big ideas here and what is the relationship between them?" Then we work to create a statement that generalizes and synthesizes what we want students to know.

Essential Questions

Essential questions are overarching questions about content and issues that guide our inquiries. They emerge from the enduring understandings and guide our planning, structure, and student learning. Essential questions help unpack an enduring understanding at the beginning and offer a place of return, so we take stock of what we've learned at the end.

Jay McTighe and Grant Wiggins (2013) offer seven defining characteristics of a good essential question.

A good essential question:

1. Is *open-ended*; that is, it typically will not have a single, final, and correct answer

2. Is *thought-provoking* and *intellectually engaging*, often sparking discussion and debate

3. Calls for *higher-order thinking*, such as analysis, inference, evaluation, prediction. It cannot be effectively answered by recall alone

4. Points toward *important, transferable* ideas within (and sometimes across) disciplines

5. Raises *additional questions* and sparks further inquiry

6. Requires *support* and *justification*, not just an answer

7. *Recurs* over time; that is, the question can and should be revisited again and again.

Here are some of the essential questions that anchor inquiries in this resource:

Science—2nd grade
Essential Questions for Living Things and Their Environments

- What is a habitat?
- How do adaptations (physical features, behaviors) help animals survive in their habitats?
- What are challenges to animals' survival?

Social Studies and History—5th grade
Essential Questions for Voice and Vote

- What is voice and in what ways do people express their voices?
- How is a vote an expression of voice?
- Who has or has not had the right to vote? Why?
- What have people been willing to do to get that right?
- How has the expression of voice effected change?

Questions to Consider When Planning an Inquiry

After determining the essential questions and enduring understandings that frame and provide the overall arc of the inquiry, we design specific lessons and experiences. As we think through where the inquiry is going and what the students do to get there, we find it helpful to ask ourselves questions like these:

Setting Overall Goals: *What do we expect kids to learn and understand by the end of this inquiry?*

- What do we want students to understand as they go about learning? What will they be able to do, create, present, or take away?
- How will the inquiry (both the topics and research process) encompass standards and curricular goals?
- How can the inquiry process support students to deepen their research and take it beyond the classroom?
- How will we ensure that kids feel ownership of the both the content and the research process?
- How will kids contribute to the direction the inquiry takes? How will we honor their questions?

Planning the Inquiry Arc: *How will kids move toward the end goals each day?*

- How much time do we have?
- What types of experiences will give students an opportunity to actively engage with the materials and resources?
- In what order do we introduce concepts and ideas?
- What we will teach/what will students do in Immerse, Investigate, Coalesce, and Take Public?
- Where can we build in time for student choice and interest to guide learning?

Gathering Resources: *What materials do we need to be successful with this inquiry?*

- Are resources varied and engaging—including books, websites, videos, infographics, articles and magazines, images, artifacts primary sources—and are they accessible for kids?
- Do they support students' enthusiasm and spark their curiosity?
- How do the resources address the enduring understandings and essential questions that frame the inquiry?
- Are the resources up-to-date and accurate and do they encourage a variety of perspectives and opinions?

Teaching Strategies: *What skills and strategies do kids need to accomplish our goals?*

- What reading, thinking, and writing strategies will students need to access and build knowledge about the content?
- What strategies and skills do they already have that we will build upon and apply to our learning?
- What new strategies and skills will they need to learn?
- What research strategies will support investigation?
- What language structures and communication strategies will open meaningful conversations?
- What knowledge and experiences will students need to ponder and respond to essential questions?
- What collaborative strategies will facilitate students to learn from each other as the inquiry unfolds?

Showing Learning: *How will kids demonstrate their learning throughout the inquiry?*

- In what ways will students share their understandings and learning over the course of the inquiry?
- What will students need to know and be able to do to complete the products, projects, and presentations that they will use to demonstrate and share new learning?
- How will kids find their way into writing, drawing, and creating to express their learning and thinking?
- What forms of artistic expression, writing, and oral language will enable them to demonstrate understanding?
- What presentation skills will students need to understand and practice to share learning and teach/inform others?

CORE PRACTICES AND LESSONS FOR RESEARCHER'S WORKSHOP

Throughout this book, we distinguish between a practice and a lesson. Practices are overarching routines that infuse all of the teaching we do. Lessons are a bit more specific. In the researcher's workshop, for instance, we define a lesson as instruction in a specific comprehension or research strategy, such as reading to answer a question or connecting the new to the known.

We begin with a core set of practices and lessons (listed below) when launching researcher's workshop. These lessons and practices are repeated throughout our inquiries so that kids internalize them over time and make them their own. We revisit practices and lessons throughout the inquiry process whether launching researcher's workshop for the first time, guiding kids in subsequent inquiries, or turning them loose to research independently.

The next chapter, "Reading and Writing in Support of Inquiry," offers additional practices and lessons in building reading independence, teaching comprehension, and writing nonfiction for different purposes. Determining your kids' needs and interests is first and foremost, so adapt any or all of these to your kids and your content. If you are interested in even more lessons, check out our Comprehension Toolkit series (Harvey and Goudvis 2016).

Practices

Co-Constructing Meaning with Interactive Read-Aloud

Asking Questions for Different Purposes

Teaching Kids How to Present Their Work

Lessons

Connect the New to the Known

Merge Thinking with New Learning

View and Read to Learn and Wonder

Annotate Text, Images, and Other Features

Take Notes to Determine Important Information and Add Thinking

Read to Find Answers

Summarize and Synthesize Information

Respond to Others' Work

PRACTICE
CO-CONSTRUCTING MEANING WITH INTERACTIVE READ-ALOUD

An interactive read-aloud is a reading practice to get at big ideas, questions, and themes. The whole process is a collaborative conversation, guided by the teacher. We find compelling, engaging picture books that are all about the big ideas, themes, and issues we want to teach. Prior to reading aloud the book, we design questions for discussion that highlight the most important ideas that we want kids to think about. We show how we stop and consider important questions and big ideas as we read. We bring kids into the discussion along the way, posing questions that will get them to think. This is reading for both understanding and enjoyment. The teacher models ways to think, talk, jot, and draw. Then students have a go, too, jotting and drawing their thinking on Post-its or in a journal.

In interactive read-alouds related to inquiries, we find books that speak to the essential questions and enduring understandings that guide the inquiry. That's why our inquiries often begin with an anchor text that thoughtfully encapsulates the big ideas. As the conversation unfolds, kids build their knowledge by listening to others and we relish their comments and insights. Ideas are discussed, lingering questions surface. We keep a record of our conversation on an anchor chart, which kids contribute to by writing and drawing their thinking and responses. The anchor chart is a way to connect and remember important ideas and make visible what we are learning as we keep the focus on enduring understandings and essential questions.

Teaching with an Interactive Read-Aloud

In an interactive read-aloud, we

- slow down and peel back the layers of our thinking to show kids how we listen to our inner conversation and jot down our thinking
- monitor comprehension, go back in the text to reread and clarify information; we may address misconceptions and how our thinking changed throughout the text
- highlight important concepts and ideas and discuss these with kids
- pose focus questions about important concepts and ideas to guide kids' thinking and foster conversation and discussion
- pause during reading to discuss and jot down new vocabulary and concepts
- discuss kids' original thoughts and insights
- link central concepts back to the essential questions and enduring understandings.

Language for Interactive Read-Alouds

This makes me think about _____.

I wonder _____.

Hmm, that's interesting. I never knew that _____.

Wait. I have a question. (Why? What? How? When? Where?)

What are you thinking and wondering about?

Who has an idea about _____?

I have some background knowledge about that.

I didn't quite get that. Let me reread it.

Here's a challenging word. It means _____.

What do you think is the big idea here?

I'm thinking this is a really important idea/concept/theme.

Let's discuss what it means.

Say more about that.

How has your thinking changed?

What are you thinking now?

PRACTICE
ASKING QUESTIONS FOR DIFFERENT PURPOSES

Inquiry is all about honoring kids' questions and teaching them to expand their questioning repertoire. Questions that are open-ended, authentic, and don't have easy answers drive the research process. We teachers model questions for many different purposes throughout the inquiry process. The chart below lists different kinds of questions and language that supports kids to ask them.

We ask questions to	Language for asking questions
● Seek accurate information and build knowledge.	What . . . ? Did . . . ? Who . . . ? When . . . ? What is happening? What did you learn about . . . ?
● Seek explanations.	Why . . . ? How . . . ? How do you know . . . ? How can we explain . . . ?
● Consider what might happen; encourage supposition and creative thinking.	What if . . . ? What might happen if . . . ? How might things have turned out differently?
● Solicit opinions and thinking.	What do you think? Do you agree or not? Who has a different idea? Can you say more about . . . ?
● Summarize and synthesize information.	What are the big ideas here? What information is important to remember? How is your knowledge/ thinking changing?
● Express empathy and perhaps take action.	I can't imagine . . . Why is this happening? How does this make you feel? What can we do about this? Is there a way to get involved?
● Challenge information; seek evidence.	How do you know? What is the evidence for . . . ? What might be another reason for . . . ?
● Seek out multiple perspectives.	What would be a different way of thinking about this? Whose perspective is not being considered here? Whose voice is not being heard?
● Tie information back to essential questions. Transfer questions to other topics.	What is the relationship between . . . ? How does this relate to our essential question . . . ?

PRACTICE TEACHING KIDS HOW TO PRESENT THEIR WORK

Kids share work. Sharing and presenting is a very valuable skill. Notice how adults speak with their presentations. Are they presenting in a group? How is the group working together? Do speakers involve the audience? When kids take learning and thinking public, all these are considerations.

Presenting with a team of diverse thinkers and researchers happens often. Kids work in research teams of two to four in a group. The team decides who will begin then who speaks next. Everyone has a chance to talk and explain.

Learning to present is a process and takes time. One thing we do know: The more opportunities we have to speak to a group, the more comfortable we are. We learn how to prepare and also to speak on the spot or extemporaneously. We think about and learn to be responsive to an audience. Kids learn language that frames their explanations and encourages discussion.

Questions and Considerations for Speakers

Where should I stand?

How loudly or softly should I speak?

How long should I speak?

How do I get the audience involved? (turn and talk)

What do I need to do to set up? (easel, clipboards, Post-its, pens, online sources, projector)

What drawings or videos will I show or explain?

What information will I read and what will I explain?

Who will begin the presentation?

What do I do when the group turns and talks?

What are the three or four things we are going to explain and focus on?

How long will our presentation be?

Language for Sharing and Teaching

Stand to the side of your work so the audience can see it.

1. We studied _____.
2. We were wondering about _____ so we wanted to learn more. Turn and talk about what you think you know about _____.
3. Some cool and interesting things I learned were _____.
4. After we learned some more we had a lot of questions.
5. Some of our questions are _____.
6. We drew a lot too. This drawing shows _____.
7. If you want to learn more, you might like to read these books _____.
8. Questions, comments, and connections?
9. Please turn and talk about what you think about _____ and jot and draw on your Post-it.
10. Who would like to share their thinking?
11. Please come and post your comments on my work. Remember, if you want to study _____, too, you can read these books and use these online sources.

LESSON Connect the New to the Known

Purpose The background knowledge we bring to our reading colors every aspect of our learning. Readers need to connect what they already know to their new learning in meaningful ways. When kids share what they think they know, this leaves open the possibility that their thinking may change as they learn new information. We explain what misconceptions are—so kids are prepared to change their thinking if need be. Understanding what kids bring in terms of background knowledge guides our teaching.

Engage Kids jot and draw what they already know on Post-its, which we add to an anchor chart headed What We Think We Know About _____. This provides a record of kids' thinking and learning over time. One thought: to ensure everyone can contribute to the conversation, we sometimes watch a short video or respond to a photograph to jump-start kids' thinking. In this way, everyone can share something they already know, even if they just observed it in the video or image.

Model/Guide Good readers think about what they already know about a topic before we begin reading. When we pay attention to what we already know about a topic and connect this to new information we are learning, our reading makes more sense.

"Notice how I think about what I think I already know. I'll record my background knowledge on this Post-it and put it up on our chart. But as we watched that video about _____, I was thinking the information I was hearing is different from what I already knew. I had what we call a misconception. A misconception is something we think we know, but it actually turns out that our information isn't accurate. I thought (*share misconception*) but now I'm thinking about the more accurate information I just read. I'll cross out what I used to think and put the new information I just learned on a Post-it."

Practice Now we tell the kids it's their turn. They will draw and jot information they think they know about _____ on their own Post-its. We put these Post-its up on the chart.

Share When the kids come back together, we ask who would like to share out some background knowledge they have. As kids continue to learn new information, they may return to the original chart and correct their initial misconceptions, noting more accurate information and how their thinking changed. We provide the language they will need to talk about how their thinking changed as they read, listened to information, or viewed it:

My thinking changed _____.

I used to think _____, but now I know _____.

Now I understand that _____.

LESSON Merge Thinking with New Learning

Purpose Readers need to merge their thinking with what they learn from the text to better understand and remember it. We introduce the idea of the reader's "inner voice," a voice that signals them to stop, think, and respond when they meet new information.

Engage We read a few pages of a picture book, or share a short excerpt of a text with features, and ask kids to turn and talk about what they notice or see. We then point out that we are in fact merging our thinking with what we read and notice in the text. We share a definition of merged thinking: Merged thinking happens when we combine our own thinking with the images, words, and other features of the text to learn something new.

Model/Guide Kids sit up close with clipboards and Post-its. We continue reading and viewing to learn new information.

"When we read nonfiction, we are reading to learn. As I read, I am going to share what my 'inner voice' is saying as I read. My inner voice is a voice in my head that might say something like, 'That's interesting, I never knew that before!' or 'Wow! I was surprised to find out that …' Watch me read and merge my thinking with new learning. I'll ask you to share out what you noticed me doing. (*After teacher modeling, kids turn and talk and share out what they noticed.*)

"I just noticed some new information about _____. Here's how I'll say it in my own words. Then I really understand it. So I'll say, 'I never knew _____.' I'm going to stop and think about this new learning and then jot it down. I'll draw a little sketch here, too, to show my new learning.

"Here's our chart of language that signals new learning. We might hear our inner voice say …"

Language That Signals New Learning	
I never knew _____.	I noticed _____.
I learned _____.	I didn't know _____.
I was surprised to find out that _____.	Now I'm thinking _____.

"Now it's your turn. Talk, jot down, and draw something new that you learned as we read and viewed just now."

Practice Kids write and illustrate their new learning as they view images or read their own book or article. They use Post-its as they refer to the Language That Signals New Learning chart to support them as they talk about how they merge their thinking with new learning.

Share As kids share out their new learning, we encourage them to use that language to show how they are merging their thinking with new information. We also prompt them to write new information in their own words. Writing and drawing about concepts in their own words solidifies kids' understanding.

LESSON View and Read to Learn and Wonder

Purpose With a provocative website, article, or video, kids can't help but notice new information. When they learn something new, they often wonder about it. We illustrate how new and engaging information often sparks us to ask a question.

Engage A startling image or surprising information hooks kids immediately, and they discuss their reactions by turning and talking. Questions surface, and we point out that new and amazing information often prompts questions.

Model/Guide Using an I learned/I wonder chart, we model how to jot and draw new learning as we read. Often a question follows hot on the heels of new information.

> "I learned some amazing information right here. I'll write it on my Post-it. (*Writes and sketches.*) But now that I stop to think about it, I'm wondering _____. I'll jot my question down right next the information I learned. Go ahead and turn and talk about the information.
>
> "What are some questions you have? Remember that you can take a look at our question words, listed right up here on the chart. I see several of you have questions. Let's put your questions right up here on the chart next to mine. Now I'll keep reading, and you can jot down what you learn on a Post-it. Remember to mark it with an *L* because it is information you learned. If you have a question, jot that down, too. You could mark it with . . . (*Kids shout out, 'A question mark!'*)"

Practice Kids may put their new learning on the outside of a folded paper, with the question written inside, creating a pop-up booklet.

Share We co-construct an anchor chart where kids can share their questions and possible answers, encouraging them to link the information they are learning back to the big concepts.

Take It Further Using this process for generating questions, kids apply the strategy in their independent reading and begin to record and explore their own questions.

LESSON Annotate Text, Images, and Other Features

Purpose Annotating, or leaving tracks of thinking, includes asking questions, jotting and drawing thinking, and recording new learning. Reacting and responding to information encourages discussion and engagement with the text.

Engage We project or give kids a copy of a section of an article, an image, or a feature such as a diagram. To launch the conversation, we ask kids to turn, talk, and discuss their responses and reactions. Listening in, we point out the variety of strategies they used to respond: asking questions, reacting to new information, inferring from features and images.

Model/Guide We project a section of text, an image, a feature, or a combination of these and show how we

- Record new information in your own words: "*I'm going to put what I just read into my own words and write it right next to those words in the text. I'm paraphrasing the information, which helps me remember it.*"

- Pose a question: "*This part confused me a little. I have a question. Then I'll read on and perhaps when I learn more I'll be able to answer my question.*"

- Infer from words or images: "*This photograph is really interesting. Maybe it explains . . . I'm inferring that . . . I don't know for sure so perhaps reading the text will confirm my inference.*"

- Think through a diagram: "*I'm going to jot down what I learned from this diagram. I'll put my thinking and learning right next to it.*"

- Figure out a puzzling part: "*I read on, or reread, or pay special attention to images or features when I'm confused.*"

We then let kids go to read and annotate on their own, reminding them that when we annotate, we are jotting down what our inner voice is saying to us as we read.

Practice We create a chart of the possibilities for annotating texts: questions, inferences, thinking, reactions, sketches, and so on. Kids continue to read on their own or with a partner or tackle another piece of text or an image, leaving tracks of their thinking and learning.

Share Kids come together to share their annotations and we add to the chart with other ways to leave tracks of thinking.

Take It Further Kids can extend annotations to different platforms (digital annotation, for example) or kinds of texts (infographics or timelines, for example) that require tweaking the way we annotate. We reflect as a group on the strategies they used to record their thinking and new learning.

LESSON Take Notes to Determine Important Information and Add Thinking

Purpose We demonstrate how to navigate texts, using headings and other features as clues to the important information we want to remember. We always add a column for thinking because when we think about information, we are more likely to learn and remember it.

Engage Kids take a look at a magazine, an online article, or another short text, using the images, title, headings, captions, and features to figure out and discuss what it's about. We introduce a two-column note-taking scaffold, which has Important Information in the left-hand column and My Thinking in the right-hand column.

Model/Guide "What do you think? What is this article about? What clues did you get from the photos, captions, and other features?" (*We discuss.*) "Headings often indicate important information, so what's important is _____."

"Now I'll put the information into my own words and write it in the left-hand column. Putting information into my own words means that I really understand it. I've got some thoughts about this, so I'll add my thinking in the right-hand column. I'm thinking _____. When I think about the information, I'm more likely to remember it. If I have a question, I'll jot that in the My Thinking column. When we learn something new, we often wonder about it and our questions are important."

Practice The kids take notes on the rest of the article, putting information into their own words and responding to it in the My Thinking column.

Share Kids come together to share out important information and thinking with the whole group. Sometimes kids meet in groups of four to share out, so everyone has a chance to share.

LESSON Read to Find Answers

Purpose Navigating a variety of sources enables kids to answer their questions. We demonstrate how to read to find an answer in an article, in this case using headings to navigate the text. With books we'd use a table of contents. With an online article we'd search for specific answers.

Engage We look over the article (or text as a whole). Kids have a chance to notice the photographs, captions, headings, and information in the text. We point out helpful features—words in bold, sections with headings, images and captions, diagrams, and so on—and how they help us navigate text. We also discuss the article's title and the big idea(s).

Model/Guide We model how to skim and scan an article to see how we might find information that answers our question(s). Maybe we have to infer information from the text or headings, so we guide kids to do this. We often use the Information/My Thinking scaffold as we read with a question in mind.

"I'm going to take a look at the headings and see if they signal information that would help me answer our question(s). Listen to this heading; I think it will help us answer our question because it is about _____.

"I'll look at the photographs and captions, because they will give me a sense of what's going on in the text. Here I see _____, which relates to my question, so I'll look more closely at the image and read the caption.

"Let's read the first part of the article and see if we can find some answers to our question. Remember that we are always merging our thinking with new information—that's how we really come to understand it and remember it! Watch me as I write the new information in the column labeled New Information. Then I'll add my thinking in the My Thinking column. Maybe I have another question or a response or connection to the information. I can write all those thoughts right here.

"Now it's your turn—let's make sure we have written the question at the top of our note-taking page so we can keep it in mind as we read."

Practice Kids work in pairs or independently to continue reading the text, keeping the question(s) in mind. They can also read to find answers to questions they come up with.

Share Kids come back together and share possible answers to their question(s).

Take It Further Add to the chart of search strategies for answering questions. Kids use this as they answer their own questions and engage further research.

LESSON Summarize and Synthesize Information

Purpose Kids learn different ways to express their new learning and make it comprehensible to a reader or viewer, writing and drawing to inform and teach others.

Engage Using examples done previously, we show kids how they can work big. They collect a variety of Post-its, sketches, and notes, all of which are organized on large paper. Another possibility is a mind map, with a topic or central question written in the middle of a large piece of paper. Stems or arms that include information on various aspects of the topic or question spiral out from the center.

Model/Guide We model how to organize and illustrate new learning on a poster and a mind map:

"I'm going to think through how to organize what I've learned. Here are some features that will help communicate what I want to say. They include maps, close-ups, cutaways, and diagrams. I could also add a glossary to define important words and a list of the sources I used. You can see that my poster has three big ideas. I'll put all the information that relates to _____ on this section. And all the information that relates to _____ right here. And I'll write about _____ and add an illustration that shows this information. Sometimes a picture tells us more than words. I want to do a close-up of _____ because it will really show what _____ looks like.

   "Now I will demonstrate how to create a mind map. I'll begin by writing my topic in the middle and illustrating it, too. I am thinking there are three big ideas about _____ that I want to share, so I'll sketch three stems, or arms, coming out from the center. On this first stem, I'll include information about _____. I'll sketch another stem and color it _____ because it is about _____. I'll do a third stem for my third big idea and label it _____. Now I can add illustrations that show the information. This is a way to make my information engaging so people will want to read and view it."

Practice We remind kids to talk with a partner or friend about their plan for the poster or mind map before they begin to draw and sketch. Then they begin to work on it.

Share Kids may not finish their posters or mind maps in one session, but we share our in-progress work and thinking. We tape in-progress or finished projects to the wall or put them on easels, so kids can move around the room and respond with comments and questions. What better way to get feedback on these works in progress? (For more information on mind maps, check out #mindmaps.)

LESSON Respond to Others' Work

Purpose Scientists and researchers often share their work with others—at conferences and seminars, and as they collaborate together. As students share their work and teach others what they have learned, they expect to receive thoughtful comments and questions from their peers and adults, too. Teaching kids respectful and thoughtful language for responding to another's work is an important part of the learning process.

Engage Kids come up to present their work. The audience is ready to respond with clipboards and Post-its, primed to connect, question, and comment on what is being shared. To energize the audience, we remind them that sharing is really important. We are *all* teachers and learners!

Model/Guide "_____ and _____ are going to share right now. You each have Post-its so you are ready to respond with writing and drawing. Be sure to listen carefully and this team will stop partway through their sharing and give you a chance to jot and draw your thoughtful responses or ask questions.

"When they are finished, we'll take some time to share out your responses to their work. They'll ask if you have any questions, comments, or connections. Remember, connections in this case are ideas and experiences that relate to _____ and _____'s topic.

"You can also give the team positive comments. What would those sound like? (*Kids respond with some possibilities: 'I like your drawing because it shows so much detail.'*) That's great thinking—you are right on. Remember you want to give specific feedback about the work—not simply say, 'I like your drawing.'

"And don't forget to ask questions that you might be wondering about. We learn so much from each of you—and this is a good time to think about questions that you, our specialists, can answer!"

Practice Give kids a chance to talk and respond on their Post-its after each group presents. Each team or individual has a chance to be both a teacher and a learner.

Share Once we have shared out each child's or team's work, we wrap up the session by asking kids to reflect on what they have learned from one another and how their thinking has changed. We return to the essential questions and enduring understandings, asking kids to share how their thinking has changed through the research process.

Launching Inquiry

At the beginning of the year, we spend time establishing the foundation for ongoing researcher's workshop. As with every inquiry, we attend to both content (the topic and discipline under study) and the process (the recursive steps we go through to teach the research process).

We design enduring understandings and essential questions that set the direction of the inquiry. To build intrigue in the topic, we choose diverse resources that

- build kids' excitement and curiosity about the topic
- are accessible to all kids and responsive to their varying experiences and background knowledge
- represent a variety of media, appealing to different learning styles
- inspire deep dives into content spin-offs.

We explicitly teach the lessons in each part of the inquiry framework—Immerse, Investigate, Coalesce, and Take Public—and go through the inquiry process as a class, modeling each of the launching practices and lessons.

To support you in launching your own inquiry, up next are

- a generic framework for a launching inquiry
- an overview of Brad's launching inquiry: Living Things and Their Environments
- how Brad teaches the core lessons and practices as this inquiry unfolds in his classroom.

Generic Framework for Launching Inquiries

IMMERSE

Teachers

- flood the room with resources and show kids where and how to find them
- introduce enduring understandings (EUs) and essential questions (EQs)
- activate and assess background knowledge (BK)
- engage kids in read-alouds/exploration to build intrigue
- model their own curiosity and passions

Students

- explore resources and connect these to their lives and experiences
- engage with compelling content and questions that spark intrigue and interest
- develop familiarity with topic, activate BK
- begin to record (write, talk, draw) responses, questions, information, and thinking

INVESTIGATE

Teachers

- model merging thinking with information
- tie information and thinking to enduring understandings and essential questions
- demonstrate when we learn something new, we might ask questions about it
- demonstrate how to leave tracks of learning and thinking: jotting digitally and in print, drawing
- model how to ask authentic questions and pursue interests

Students

- read, write, talk, and draw information and concepts; merge with BK
- learn new information and wonder about it
- leave tracks/annotate by talking, writing, drawing
- ask and research authentic questions
- develop a sense of agency about the research process

You can use this generic framework for launching an inquiry on any content or topic. You can note how the generic lessons (pp. 51–58) play out in each part of the framework. The following inquiry on the environment is simply an example of a launching inquiry with specific content.

COALESCE

Teachers

- revisit EUs and EQs and tie to information and new learning
- model how to summarize and synthesize information using a variety of response options
- model how to summarize and synthesize big ideas and important information

Students

- review their Post-its, information, and questions
- practice ways to summarize and organize information through talk, writing, and artistic expression
- begin to apply research strategies to related topics and questions
- create many forms of projects—digital, artistic, dramatic—to demonstrate learning

TAKE PUBLIC

Teachers

- establish expectations for sharing
- teach the language of sharing/presenting
- demonstrate how to present information in engaging ways

Students

- understand the purpose of sharing: to teach and feel empowered
- learn language for sharing/presenting and responding
- become confident presenters by engaging peers in conversation and dialogue
- use talk, writing, and artistic expression to share ideas and information

Launching Inquiry Overview in Brad's Classroom

This example of a launching inquiry develops some of the key themes in Brad's science curriculum—the relationship between animals and their environments. He introduces kids to the research process with a concrete topic that engages kids and gets them thinking about the larger issues related to animal habitats, adaptations, and survival.

Inquiry Topic   Living Things and Their Environments

Enduring Understandings

As we learn about the amazing and wondrous aspects of all living things, we come to more fully understand nature and our world.

Knowledge about all living things and how they are adapted to and survive in their habitats make us more thoughtful caretakers of our environment.

Essential Questions for Each Lesson

1. What is a habitat?
2. How do adaptations (physical features, behaviors, and so on) help animals survive in their habitats?
3. What are challenges to animal survival?

Immerse

Introduce enduring understandings and essential questions with an interactive read-aloud

Practice: Co-Constructing Meaning with Interactive Read-Aloud

* Read aloud *Each Living Thing*, respond orally and in writing with poetry snippets to create a poetry spiral. Introduce the enduring understandings.

Connect the new to the known to activate background knowledge

Lesson: Connect the New to the Known

* Record "what we think we know" about bats to ascertain and activate kids' background knowledge. Tie background knowledge back to the essential questions about adaptations and survival to see the bigger picture.

Investigate

Merge thinking with new information

Lesson: Merge Thinking with New Learning

* Read and respond to the book *Little Lost Bat* to build knowledge about bats' physical features, behaviors, and adaptations. Emphasize concepts that apply to both bats and other animals children know about.

View and read to record thinking and ask questions

Lesson: View and Read to Learn and Wonder

* Ask questions and record new learning from a website on bats.

Annotate text to respond to new information

Lesson: Annotate Text, Images, and Other Features

* Jot new learning, questions, and inferences by leaving tracks of thinking on an article. Encourage kids' flexible use of annotation strategies to understand information.

Brad teaches each of the practices and lessons for launching an inquiry here. Most of these lessons (pp. 51–58) teach comprehension strategies as tools for reading, writing, and research. See "Reading and Writing in Support of Inquiry" for additional comprehension and writing lessons.

Resources

Each Living Thing by Joanne Ryder

Little Lost Bat by Sandra Markle

Magazine articles and other picture books about bats

Bat Conservation International website

Image collection

Bat Rescue website

Coalesce

Summarize and synthesize information and ideas

Lesson: Summarize and Synthesize Information

* Create posters with illustrations and nonfiction features. Look for kids' excitement and ownership in the process.

Generalize concepts across texts and topics

* Encourage kids to explore and share related topics that excite them.

Make and create to demonstrate learning

* Create models and replicas of bat environments, bat behaviors, and a bat rescue operation. Celebrate kids' multimodel expression when working in three dimensions.

Take Public

Share and present new learning

Practice: Teaching Kids How to Present Their Work

* Teach presentation skills and strategies for sharing projects. Give kids plenty of practice participating actively as an audience.

* Class discussions circle back to address essential questions and enduring understandings.

IMMERSE

To launch researcher's workshop, we flood the room with topic-related resources and begin with a whole-group activity. Options include videos, an interactive website, or an interactive read-aloud, so that we capture kids' attention and introduce key ideas related to the topic.

■ Introduce enduring understandings and essential questions with an interactive read-aloud

See Practice "Co-Constructing Meaning with Interactive Read-Aloud," page 48

We introduce essential questions and enduring understandings with a book that focuses on a significant message—the importance of valuing and respecting all living things. Introducing the inquiry with the picture book *Each Living Thing* captures an enduring understanding—the interdependence of all living things. It focuses on observing wildlife and respecting all living things. As we read, the children make connections to their background knowledge about habitats and animals that live in them. They respond and react to the descriptive language of the text and create their own short snippets or small poems.

When we coteach, kids observe our conversation about the text, just as they will have conversations about the text with their peers.

Teachers model their responses to the text, then kids have a go at writing their own responses.

We're going to be studying different animals and learning how they live in their habitats, how they are adapted to their environments, and how they survive dangers and other threats. Think for a moment about an animal you know about—turn and talk about how you think it survives in its habitat—the environment where it lives. (*Kids turn and talk and then share out briefly.*)

Let's think about some essential questions about animals that we will explore together as we read these books. I've written them up here:

- – How do animals adapt to and survive in their habitats?
- – What is a habitat?
- – Which adaptations (physical features, behaviors) help animals survive?
- – What are challenges to their survival?

We'll begin our inquiry with an interactive read-aloud with this book, *Each Living Thing*. Take a look at the cover. Turn and talk about what you see, what you notice. (*Kids share out.*)

As I read, think about the words and ideas and pay close attention to the illustrations. Here's a chart of what we hear the voice in our head say when we stop to think and react as we listen to a story or read a book on our own.

WHAT WE DO	LANGUAGE OF THINKING
Think about what we are hearing, seeing, and feeling	This makes me think about _____.
	I can hear _____.
	I see _____.
	I feel _____.
Wonder and ask questions	I wonder . . .
	Why _____? What ____?
	How _____? Who _____?
	Where _____? When _____?
Connect to our background knowledge and experiences	I have a connection to _____.
	This reminds me of _____.
	I have some background knowledge about _____.
	I know a lot about _____.

(Read aloud.)

> Be careful of snapping crabs and swooping gulls,
> of stinging jellyfish afloat and free
> of alligators slyly drifting by . . .
> and giant turtles circling in the sea.

> Let's stop and talk about what you are wondering, thinking, and visualizing as well as connections to your own experiences. *(Kids share out.)*

> The important message in this book is that all living things are interdependent. Let's talk about what interdependent means. *(We discuss the idea that every living thing needs other living things to survive.)*

We continue to read the book more slowly, stopping every few pages so kids can act out the descriptive language from the book. They jump as toads do, slither like snakes, step over ants, swoop like gulls. We hoot like owls, cry like seagulls. We talk about the message of the whole book—to take care of each living thing, to be watchful, to observe quietly, to respect all living things and let them be.

> Now it's your turn. You can choose one or more of the animals we read about and write your own small poem—we call it a *snippet*. A snippet is a little bit of descriptive language. Then you can illustrate your snippet.

As kids share their snippets, we put them together into a cascading poem, suspended from the ceiling and twirling in the breeze.

Snippets kids create about animals in *Each Living Thing.*

Acting out descriptive language engages kids, and there's no better way to make sure they understand it.

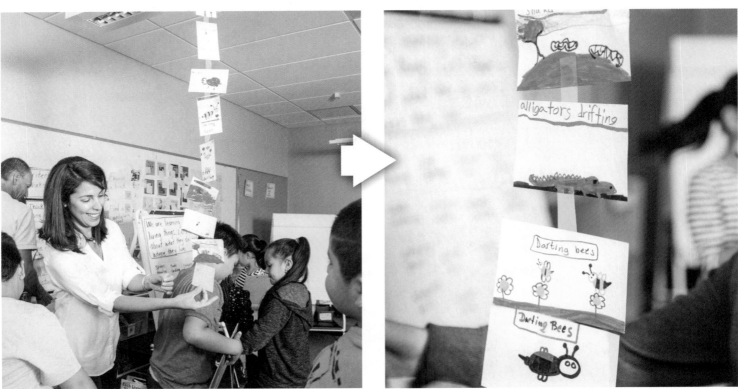

Kids create a cascading poem to share their snippets.

Next we immerse kids in knowledge about a specific animal, the bat: its physical features, behaviors, and habitats. The information they learn ensures kids genuinely understand how one particular animal is adapted to and survives in its habitat. But before we dive into texts and resources, we ascertain what kids know so they can connect what they already know to new learning. While we happened to choose bats to study, any animal works. Since the enduring understandings and the essential questions are the same for any animal, we flood the room with books, articles, and resources about many different animals because once kids grasp concepts about adaptation and survival, they broaden their understanding by reading about and exploring other animals and species.

■ Connect the new to the known to activate background knowledge

See Lesson "Connect the New to the Known," page 51

Before we begin reading, kids talk, write, and draw what they think they know about the physical features, behaviors, and habitats of bats. We create charts to capture initial background knowledge and understandings and tackle the idea that our thinking changes as we build our knowledge store—so that we can discuss kids' misconceptions when they arise.

Anchor chart What We Think We Know About Bats where we collect kids' Post-its.

INVESTIGATE

Now that kids' attention and enthusiasm are focused on a topic, we begin exploration in earnest. During the investigation phase, kids delve into multiple sources and learn strategies for accessing, questioning, and re-membering important information. Curiosity sparks ongoing questions.

■ Merge thinking with new information

See Lesson "Merge Thinking with New Learning," page 52

We begin reading books that focus on important concepts that are framed by the essential question: How do animals adapt to and survive in their habitats? We read *Little Lost Bat* by Sandra Markle because it highlights how bats adapt to and survive in various habitats. We model how to merge thinking with new information and kids respond on Post-its, jotting down and drawing different features and behaviors. We tie this knowledge back to the big ideas and essential questions.

On this chart, Teaching Science Concepts with Read-Alouds, kids record their learning and questions as they merge their thinking with new information.

Vocabulary and concepts from the book *Little Lost Bat* build knowledge about bat habitats.

When the mother bat has to leave her tiny baby to go off and hunt for food, kids are incredulous and have many questions. We ask them to share out what they learned as well as their questions.

Louisa I never knew that—right after the baby is born the mother leaves it to go hunt for food! I think the baby is going to die!

Gaia I wonder. How can the baby live by itself when it is so young?

Todd I'm confused. Where does she leave it? It really didn't say.

Gaia Let's reread. . . . It says the babies huddle together. But it doesn't say where they are.

Tina The mother bats were hanging from the ceiling. Maybe babies do that too, right after they are born.

Tommy It says the mom leaves to find food.

Ari That's how they live. If the mom didn't go out and get food so they could eat, they'd both die.

Todd But I want to find out if the baby bats hang there. We need to do some research!

By merging their thinking with the information, kids acquire concepts about survival by understanding clear examples of adaptations and the ways in which animals survive. We also honor kids' questions, making a list of questions they can explore. Wrapping up the read-aloud, kids marvel that the "abandoned" baby bat survived.

Tommy I was so surprised that the baby bat lived! The new bat nursed it just in time.

Gaia I used to think most animals protected their babies, but the baby bats were left all alone.

Jocelyn But another bat, who had lost her own baby, took care of it!

Todd Thank goodness!

Maddie Yeah, but I learned some of those baby bats die. Here's what I wrote, "I learned that when a baby bat falls to the ground, the beetles eat the baby bats."

Gaia That's terrible.

Maddie But that's what can happen. . . .

■ View and read to record thinking and ask questions

Research and inquiry are all about the disposition to be curious and ask questions. When we learn something new, we wonder about it. Kids pose questions related to their new learning.

See Lesson "View and Read to Learn and Wonder," page 53

Modeling with a website from Bat Conservation International, we show ways to record information and ask questions when we learn some new information. We collect kids' questions on an anchor chart, and Brad summarizes the process right on the chart.

As we read, we stopped at new information to write it down. We also asked questions. This helps us keep a record of our thinking and remember the information. Our learning leads to more questions. Our unanswered questions lead us into further inquiry.

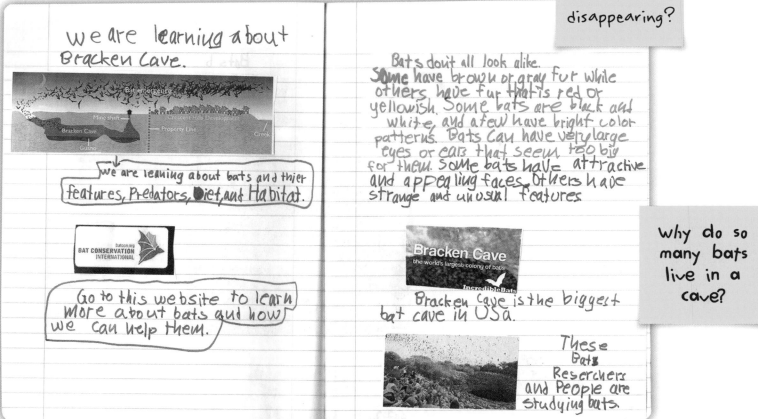

Oliver recorded notes from the website in his researcher's notebook. As he learned new information about the bats of Braken Cave, he had many questions.

■ **Annotate text to respond to new information**

Annotating text and images is one way to integrate the strategies kids have already been introduced to: accessing background knowledge, merging thinking with new information, and asking questions. As we annotate, we use these strategies as tools: responding to new information, jotting down questions, noticing how our thinking changes as we build our knowledge store.

See Lesson "Annotate Text, Images, and Other Features," page 54

As we continue our investigation, one child brings an article from home about amazing facts about bats. This voluntary literacy event becomes a classroom lesson on annotating text. We read the article in an interactive read-aloud, with the article posted on a large chart, reinforcing comprehension strategies: asking questions, reacting and responding to amazing information, and so on. The child leads a class reading of the article, and as we read it together, he demonstrates how he left tracks of thinking right on the page. When kids are teachers, everyone pays attention!

COALESCE

Organizing what they have learned about the inquiry topic requires kids to summarize and synthesize what they have found out but also revisit the big ideas and essential questions. Kids summarize their new learning on a poster, in a teaching book, with a short report, and so on—whatever makes their thinking visible so they can share it with others.

■ Summarize and synthesize information

See Lesson "Summarize and Synthesize Information," page 57

To begin to pull the Living Things and Their Environments inquiry together, we return to the essential questions to summarize and synthesize new learning:

- What is a habitat?
- Which adaptations (physical features, behaviors) help animals survive in their habitat?
- What are challenges to animal survival?

Creating a large poster is an effective way to summarize and display learning. Kids love working big. Posters are colorful and fun to create. A poster is an opportunity for kids to

- transfer and apply the EQs and EUs to their own animals
- collect their new learning—Post-its, drawings, and so on—in one place on a large chart
- choose how they will organize the information
- incorporate nonfiction features especially illustrations with labels and captions, close-ups, and so on.

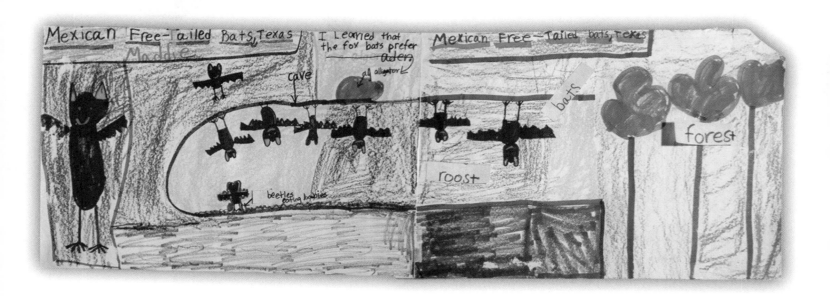

Early in the school year it is important for kids to develop ownership of their work and to get excited about ways to share their new learning. Large posters are an entry point into sharing knowledge with others—writing to inform and teach. Kids write and illustrate information, including features such as captions, labels, and close-ups that will capture readers' interest.

■ Generalize concepts across texts and topics

Kids learn that bats find their food using echolocation, and they immediately wonder if any other animals use echolocation. Checking out the library and online sources, kids find out about whales, dolphins, and other echolocators. They begin to transfer concepts they have learned about one animal to other animals. That's the point!

One child collected her Post-its, placed them on a poster, and added illustrations and information. Her parents' responses, as well as those from other adults and students, are placed right on her poster.

Kids plop down on the floor with a large pad of paper and markers, their books and iPads open to information about animal echolocators. They create a poster called Animals That Use Echolocation and share it.

Josh These are our sources. They are about dolphins and other animals.

Anna We found out that dolphins use echolocation to navigate and find food too! We were so surprised!

Ben And toothed whales use echolocation, too, just like bats.

Anna I drew a picture of a toothed whale. Here are the lines that show it using echolocation. We showed the bats and dolphins with those lines, too.

Lyla Why is there a butterfly on your poster? Do they use echolocation?

Josh No, the bat uses echolocation to find and eat the butterfly.

Ben Here are some Post-its. Please write and draw what you learned from our poster and presentation. Are there any questions, comments, or connections?

By exploring ideas and concepts in relation to other animals and topics, kids demonstrate genuine understanding about concepts and transfer this knowledge to other topics. Enthusiasm grows as they realize the power of becoming researchers.

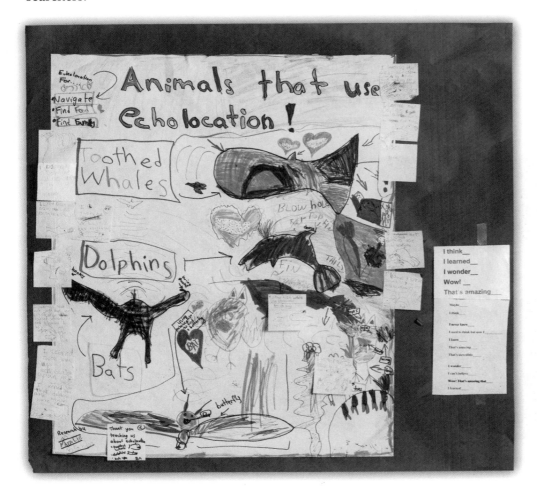

■ Make and create to demonstrate new learning

In creating real stuff, kids' understandings or misconceptions are clear. Making things provides an opportunity to discuss big concepts and ideas as kids create ways to demonstrate learning and thinking.

Kids are natural builders and makers, so they love creating museum exhibits. Legos on a shelf comprise a sort of "makerspace" in the classroom. It doesn't take kids long to see the possibilities. They are intrigued by a bat rescue center in Australia they learn about online. Here bats were nursed back to health—brought there by people who found injured bats in the wild.

Lucy Here is a house and the rescue center for bats that need help. Let's write Post-it notes to label it.

Andrew I'm going to start making some scientists looking at a cave of bats. Here's the ceiling with the bats hanging down. (*They used the bookshelf as the cave and taped the bats, created out of Legos, to the top, labeling it "bat roost."*)

David I'll make the forest on top of the bat cave. Here are the trees and the stream—and here are the bats in the forest.

Andrew I'll make scientists observing the cave, with their notebooks.

David, Andrew, and Lucy become the curators of their bat exhibit, saying, "Come on over and we'll tell you what we made!"

Imagination grounded in new learning is key. Kids express their newfound knowledge and ideas in many ways, creating spaces and habitats. As the children work, they collaboratively envision and construct scenarios that illustrate new learning.

Kids make accurate representations of a bat rescue center, an owl hunting a bat, and Mexican free-tailed bats roosting in a cave.

TAKE PUBLIC

The main purpose of taking learning public is to teach kids thoughtful ways of presenting and participating—presenting ideas and information as well as participating as attentive members of an audience.

Kids can't (and don't) wait to write and illustrate their own learning. They share their work in progress every day, keeping the "products" of their research short and simple. The focus is on teaching the research process rather than creating elaborate projects.

■ Share and present new learning

See Practice "Teaching Kids How to Present Their Work," page 50

Presenting takes practice. We teach kids how to present as well as how to be a respectful audience for others. Because they have been sharing out their work regularly, they are ready for some of the finer points of presenting—and listening to and learning from others.

We teach presenters to

- be prepared, plan what they are going to say
- be aware of their audience
- speak clearly and speak up
- look at the audience
- respond to the audience's comments and questions.

Kids share and take their thinking public in small groups, which encourages give-and-take discussion.

This child shares her many questions.

We ask listeners and responders to

- look at the presenter and pay attention
- share comments and questions when asked
- respond with their own thinking.

Discussion is at the heart of learning. We teach kids ways to respond fully and thoughtfully to one another's ideas and interact around the knowledge they have gained throughout the unit. Kids participate in many conversations about their learning throughout the study, but presenting a finished poster or piece is special.

Kids are teachers and they direct the sharing session. Everyone is listening and talking about the topic at hand. After kids have presented, the audience responds, turning and talking, offering positive comments about a child's work and thinking and, of course, asking questions. Teaching kids to ask, "Any questions, comments, or connections?" of their peers is the best conversation starter we know for kids to respond thoughtfully to one another's work. Kids discover that everyone is both a learner and a teacher.

When presenters are finished sharing, they ask, "Any questions, comments, or connections?" and kids respond.

Kids share out all sorts of projects. This child wrote a story about bats and created a museum exhibit to go with it.

Guiding Inquiry

After kids have become familiar with the research process through one or more whole-class inquiries, teachers model less and guide more. As kids develop their repertoire of research skills, they take greater responsibility for finding resources, pursuing their own investigations, and sharing their learning. Everyone's different, so we watch carefully and listen closely, offering just the right amount of scaffolding and support, reteaching core lessons as needed.

Now that students have experienced a full arc of lessons, from Immerse to Take Public, we use the inquiry framework more flexibly. We may skip Immerse when we are building on learning from a previous inquiry. We may cycle multiple times through Investigate and Coalesce, expanding our understanding. One constant is that we release kids to research on their own when they are ready.

In the Guiding Inquiry, kids add to their note-taking strategies, learning additional ways to record new information. We also demonstrate additional ways for kids to create engaging nonfiction as they summarize, synthesize, and share their learning. Check out the lessons on teaching books, field guides, brochures, and design techniques in the writing section of "Reading and Writing to Support Inquiry" (pp. 109–74) for even more ideas.

Generic Framework for Guiding Inquiry

Here is a generic framework to use with a guiding inquiry. We revisit core lessons, give kids time to practice, and introduce more options for taking notes, for example. See writing in "Reading and Writing in Support of Inquiry" for additional ways kids can summarize and synthesize information.

IMMERSE

Teachers

- support kids to find resources
- encourage kids to activate and access background knowledge
- show kids how to tie their research back to EUs and EQs
- continue to share their interest and enthusiasm for the research process

Students

- eagerly seek out and find resources for research with guidance
- build background knowledge through reading, viewing, and listening
- begin to tie their new information to enduring understandings and essential questions
- cultivate their curiosity through opportunities to explore their interests

INVESTIGATE

Teachers

- guide students to apply previously learned strategies to a related or new topic
- guide students to expand the possibilities for responding in talk, writing, and artistic expression
- guide students to ask questions that propel research and investigation

Students

- read with a question in mind
- take notes and annotate sources
- express their responses and opinions in many different ways, including digital, artistic, musical, and written expression

COALESCE

Teachers

- guide students to summarize and synthesize information and big ideas across texts and tie information to the enduring understandings and essential questions
- encourage students to see connections between and across texts
- open up possibilities for the ways in which kids can express their thinking and learning

Students

- synthesize information across texts
- create original ways to summarize and synthesize new learning
- recognize thematic connections across texts

TAKE PUBLIC

Teachers

- guide students to thoughtfully respond to one another's work
- support kids to put their work in public places
- introduce possibilities for taking action
- cycle back to consider EUs and EQs

Students

- present information, respond to it, and come to care about it
- develop their own understandings of EUs and EQs
- discuss ways to take action

Guiding Inquiry Overview in Brad's Classroom

When students have a lot of background knowledge about a topic or extensive experience with researching, it is often possible to guide an inquiry with a gentle hand, giving kids more choice and freedom. This Endangered Animals inquiry extends and builds on the information and the process kids learned through the previous inquiry (Living

Inquiry Topic ___Endangered Animals___

Enduring Understandings

There are many reasons why animals become vulnerable and possibly endangered. Learning about how humans are impacting the environment helps us better understand what is happening in the natural world.

Changes in environments and habitats affect animal life. As we investigate these changes, we learn what we can do to be better stewards of the Earth and its resources.

Essential Questions for Each Lesson

1. What happens when an animal's habitat and survival are threatened?

2. What are some of the reasons why animals are endangered?

3. What can we do about it?

Immerse

Review enduring understandings (EUs) and essential questions (EQs)

* Review concepts and information about habitats, adaptations, and survival. Tie to EQs and EUs to build background for the new inquiry topic.

Activate and ascertain background knowledge

* Activate and share background knowledge abut polar bears and the Arctic environment.

Investigate

Take notes to sort and sift information and ideas

Lesson: Take Notes to Determine Important Information and Add Thinking

* Note-taking with a magazine article: Use headings, titles, and photos to determine important information about what is happening in the Arctic.

Read or view with a question in mind

Lesson: Read to Find Answers

* Keeping a question in mind, view a video, and stop to talk, jot, and draw.

Things and Their Environments). The resources list remains fluid when we are guiding an inquiry. Kids may find and bring in relevant resources. The key is to provide enough resources in enough different media to give all kids access to the inquiry content and process.

Resources

Books:

Waiting for Ice by Sandra Markle, *Ice Bear* by Nicola Davies, *Polar Bears* by Mark Newman

Articles:

"On Thin Ice," *National Geographic Explorer*
Magazine articles related to Arctic habitat and animals

Videos:

National Geographic videos on animals, endangered animals, video.nationalgeographic.com/video/polar-bears

Website:

polarbearsinternational.org

Coalesce

Annotate text to synthesize big ideas

* Synthesize information and evidence about the threatened polar bear habitat and the declining population of polar bears. Leave tracks of thinking on a newspaper article to surface the big ideas.

Summarize and synthesize big ideas across sources

* Summarize learning from texts, videos, and websites.

* Synthesize ideas and information with the essential questions in mind.

Explore lingering questions with online interviews

* Discuss questions for online interviews with scientists.

Take Public

Present and discuss information

* Share out new learning about the changing Arctic habitat and the influences on plants and animals.

* Cycle back to address and discuss EUs and EQs.

* Discuss ways to take action.

IMMERSE

To begin a guided inquiry, we review what we have already learned. Surrounded by appropriate resources, kids connect enduring understandings and essential questions to new topics.

■ Review enduring understandings and essential questions

As we begin this inquiry, we review what we learned about animal adaptations, survival, and habitats from the launching inquiry.

> You have learned a lot about how animals adapt to their habitats and what animals need to survive. Think about bats, koalas, and other animals and what we learned about them. What are challenges to their survival?

Kids review behaviors, physical features, diet, and other characteristics of the animals they studied. They discuss dangers the animals face and how their survival is threatened, summarizing the information in relation to a new essential question: What happens when an animal's survival is threatened? Here kids talk about what they know about koalas:

> **Joaquin** I know that there was a fire in the forest and the koalas had to escape to a different part of the woods.
>
> **Luisa** Yeah, they lost their habitat.
>
> **Gerardo** But they found a new place to live.
>
> **Luisa** But it was too near where people were building houses, so that wasn't really a safe place for them.
>
> **Sydney** When their habitat disappears, it's a big problem.

> Exactly. You are all getting the big idea here: that when an animal's habitat is threatened, it can become what we call *vulnerable*—easily hurt or harmed—or even endangered. We're going to learn more about this problem. Here's another essential question: What happens when an animal's survival is threatened?

To review the original essential questions and enduring understandings about animals, kids share out information about their physical features, adaptations, and habitat, which is recorded in a mind map summary. Now they apply this knowledge in an endangered animal inquiry.

■ Activate and ascertain background knowledge

When the snow begins to fall in Colorado, it's the perfect time to journey to the Arctic, to explore a harsh and unforgiving habitat. An endless expanse of frigid ocean water, roaring winds, blowing snow, bobbing ice floes, and the occasional lumbering polar bear intrigue kids and prompt many questions.

> Now we're going to do some research about a giant mammal, the polar bear. Let's think about what we think we know about polar bears as well as their habitat, the Arctic. On the globe, the Arctic is right here—it's the area surrounding the North Pole. Notice it is all white.
>
> "Because it's solid ice," comments Joshua.

As kids share out what they think they know, we record the information on a chart entitled What We Think We Know About Polar Bears.

We create a chart recording kids' background knowledge and what they think they know about polar bears. As Tony Stead (2005) reminds us, we choose the language *what we think we know* rather than *what we know*. This way, we discover their background knowledge including misconceptions, which we address during the inquiry.

INVESTIGATE

Kids use specific strategies for reading and viewing with understanding as well as strategies like note-taking and annotation that help them record and remember important information.

■ Take notes to determine important information and add thinking

See Lesson "Take Notes to Determine Important Information and Add Thinking," page 55

Note-taking with an article from *National Geographic Explorer* magazine introduces kids to information about the essential question "What happens when an animal's survival and habitat are threatened?"

> We are going to read the article "On Thin Ice." When we think of polar bears being "on thin ice" that means that polar bears are in trouble. It means they are at risk—when we walk "on thin ice" we may break through it at any moment—so the title is a play on words that is suggesting the big idea of this article.
>
> When we read, it's important to figure out which big ideas we need to remember. This magazine article helps us do that with the title that lets us know that polar bears are in trouble. We also can view the photos here, which show what it is like for polar bears to live with less ice. Notice that huge polar bear on that tiny little ice floe! These photos confirm the big ideas in the article: that the polar bear's habitat is changing.

As we read a magazine article about the changing polar bear habitat, we demonstrate how to take notes on important information.

Organize Your Thinking as You Read

→ If the ice melts, they won't have enough ice to live on to help them catch food.

• Ice is an important part of their habitat- every animal needs a habitat to live.

• They need ice to live.

• No ice = no holes for seals to breathe, so polar bears have no place to hunt.

Let's read this first section. [*We do.*] What are some of the big ideas we found in the article? Go ahead and turn and talk about what you think is a big idea. Then we'll note them on our chart. [*Kids turn and talk.*]

I heard some of you mentioning this important idea: If the ice melts, polar bears won't have enough ice to live on, so they won't be able to catch their food. Let's write that on our chart.

Some of you also mentioned that every animal needs a habitat it can survive in, and the polar bears need ice. I'll jot that down in our notes, too. When you write your notes, be sure to put the information in your own words instead of just copying it. That shows we really understand it.

When we carefully model and organize note-taking for kids at the beginning, they have a better shot at doing this successfully on their own. Taking notes about inquiries in subject notebooks or journals keeps all the information kids are learning in one place so they can refer back to it easily.

Now it's your turn to be the scientists and read about what's happening with the polar bears and their habitat. We're going to organize our thinking in our notebooks. Remember to write the most important ideas in your own words.

Kids continue reading the article and begin taking their own notes. Then they finish the rest of the article.

When kids first learn to take notes from their reading, they need explicit modeling. After modeling note-taking on the first part of the article, kids practice on their own, putting their own take on the information.

■ Read or view with a question in mind

See Lesson "Read to Find Answers," page 56

When we read with a question in mind, we zero in on a specific research question we want to find the answer to. We teach kids to navigate informational text using the table of contents or index to find information that answers their question. Viewing with a question in mind presents special challenges. Taking notes from a fast-paced video filled with information can be challenging for young kids.

We delve deeper into the endangered animals inquiry by viewing a video and applying what we know about reading with a question in mind. First, we watch it all the way through, so kids get the general gist. Then, to make sure we grasp and jot down important information, we watch the video a few segments at a time, stopping it after some of the most salient points, jotting and drawing notes. We rely on tools like closed captions, titled segments, and a scroll bar to help stop and start the video easily or return to parts we want to watch again.

We view the video with this question in mind: How does the polar bear's body help it survive in its cold Arctic habitat? Kids answer the question in their science notebooks.

This child's notes reflect her thoughts about the question "How does the polar bear's body help (it) survive?"

View with a question in mind: How does the polar bear's body help it survive? Kids watch a video from *National Geographic Wild—Polar Bear 101*.

COALESCE

Summarizing and synthesizing new learning across texts can take many forms: annotations, notes, posters, projects, any product that makes kids' thinking visible.

■ Annotate text to synthesize big ideas

Kids come in waving the local newspaper one day, exclaiming, "There's a story about polar bears in the paper!" These young newshounds discovered it that morning, so it's a perfect opportunity to further delve into why polar bears are endangered in their habitats. Connecting real-world concerns and issues to what they are studying motivates kids to find out more.

We post the article on a large chart so we can read and annotate it together. Kids have plenty to say about this article—and several request a copy for their science notebooks, which they annotate on their own.

We annotate with a specific purpose: to understand evidence of polar bear populations dwindling due to shrinking sea ice. This evidence supports an enduring understanding and relates to the essential question, "What happens when an animal's habitat is threatened?" Although the notion of evidence in a scientific study is challenging for kids, their considerable background knowledge on this issue prepares them to understand the facts and statistics about the declining number of polar bears.

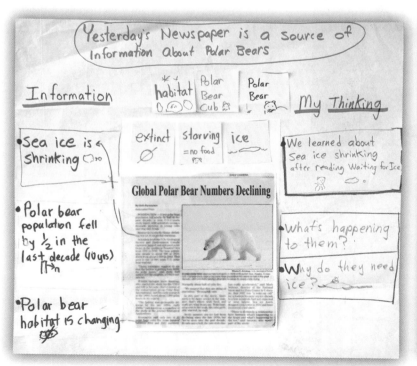

It's important that kids read real-world, challenging text—especially when they bring it into the classroom themselves.

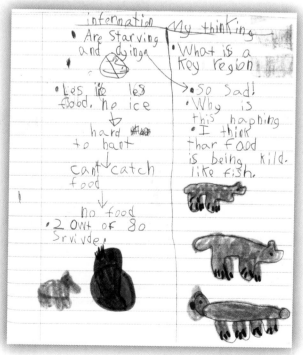

This child pasted the newspaper article in her notebook and annotated it on her own. She adds her thinking about polar bear problems: "So sad! Two out of 80 survive!"

VIDEO CLIP

Revisit and discuss essential questions and enduring understandings.

■ Summarize and synthesize big ideas across sources

Kids have deepened their understanding of issues surrounding the polar bear's changing habitat, so we return to the essential question: What happens when an animal's habitat is threatened?

Kids have gathered a lot of information from a variety of sources, so we discuss the idea that what is happening in their habitat means big changes for these giant mammals. The kids bring up information from the article "On Thin Ice," the picture book *Waiting for Ice*, the newspaper article, and online sources kids have read or viewed.

Now it's the kids' turn to summarize the information they have learned in whatever ways they choose. One child writes in her notebook:

> "Polar bear cubs are starving. I hope they find food . . . and live."

When kids share out their responses, several decide to work together to tackle what they can do to save polar bears.

Using design techniques to make their posters interactive, these students illustrate information gleaned from several sources. The seal on the poster moves through the water, surfacing just in time for the waiting polar bear to grab it.

A child synthesizes the big ideas across texts, communicating her ideas in her notebook. This child has come to care about the plight of polar bears.

Explore lingering questions with online interviews

When kids have built considerable background knowledge about a topic, they may end up with more questions than answers. As kids summarized what they had learned about polar bears, they discussed and jotted down questions they still wondered about.

They watched a video of kids asking questions of polar bear scientists, who responded with some answers.

After kids reviewed tips for interviewing, they logged on to the Polar Bears International website to submit their own questions, shown below.

TIPS FOR INTERVIEWING

Before you go online or conduct an interview, think of three questions you want to ask.

Listen carefully to the person you are interviewing.

Ask follow-up questions based on what the person is saying.

A child logs on to have an online interview with a scientist.

To see this video, enter this URL into your browser: https://www.youtube.com /watch?v=dudBiWkzQWE

VIDEO CLIP

Present
information and
take it public.

TAKE PUBLIC

Once kids develop a repertoire of different ways to present information, they choose how they will share their new learning.

■ Present and discuss information

Based on their notes from reading and viewing, a small group creates a chart of how a broken food chain affects the survival of animals living in the Arctic.

If there is no ice, the tiny plants can't grow. If there's no tiny plants, the cod that eat the plants die.

If the cod are dead, the seals and narwhals have nothing to eat and will die. If the seals and narwhals die, the polar bears will be foodless.

If polar bears are out on the ice when it melts, they may be trapped far away from land.

When the ice melts completely, the polar bears will drown.

The big ideas here become clear to kids: that all living things are interdependent, they depend on each other to survive. They respond to questions posed by the audience.

• Do you think that the polar bears can find food on land?

• What will happen to the fish if there is no krill?

• What has been happening to the polar bears' habitat?

• What can we do about this?

Supporting Independent Inquiry

Get started with independent research.

Throughout the launching and guiding inquiries, kids have solidified their understanding of ways to explore a topic as they immerse themselves in it, read to learn as they investigate it, coalesced their learning, and finally taken it public. The lessons and practices in the "Researcher's Workshop" chapter and also those in the "Reading and Writing in Support of Inquiry" chapter have become part of kids' "research repertoire." Check out lessons for coalescing and taking learning public in the writing section of "Reading and Writing in Support of Inquiry" (pp. 138–173).

Independent inquiries are just that: Kids work individually, in pairs, or in small groups, to investigate questions and topics they choose. Kids may pursue lingering questions that extend their understanding of the topics they have been learning about. Or, they may opt to investigate a brand-new topic, exploring resources, developing questions, and then reading to answer them.

When kids know a lot about a topic, they begin to care a lot, which often inspires them to action.

Generic Framework for Supporting Independent Inquiries

IMMERSE

Teachers (as needed)

- support students to find resources
- remind students to think about enduring understandings and essential questions
- know their students' topics and are on the lookout for resources

Students

- find engaging resources and activate background knowledge
- consider enduring understandings and essential questions as they read and research

INVESTIGATE

Teachers (as needed)

- support students to refine researchable questions
- review research process: asking questions, note-taking, annotation strategies, and so on

Students

- pursue their own interests and authentic questions
- continue to ask questions as they research
- apply note-taking strategies, respond as they read, listen, and view
- take the big ideas they have learned and transfer them to other topics

Just as with a construction project when you've taken the scaffolding down, if we've effectively scaffolded the launching and guiding inquiries, kids are ready to have a go on their own. Kids take the lead and we are there to support them.

COALESCE

Teachers (as needed)

- support students to understand the potential of their own ideas and original thinking
- encourage kids to transfer the information and ideas they have learned to new topics and interests

Students

- decide how they will organize, summarize, and synthesize information
- create original projects
- apply enduring understandings as they synthesize information and ideas

TAKE PUBLIC

Teachers

- provide opportunities to share research and encourage interaction around it
- support kids to consider what they can do to take effective action

Students

- present research to classmates, other classrooms, parents, the public
- actively respond to one another's work and participate in public conversations about it
- create ways to take action and advocate for a cause

Supporting Independent Inquiry Overview in Brad's Classroom

Independent inquiries require flexibility. Students' research may be about topics the class has been exploring or topics they choose. These topics emerge from something that they are passionate about or that puzzles them. We honor kids' interests and questions as they

Inquiry Topic _____?_____

Enduring Understandings

Revisit animal and environment EUs for students continuing to investigate related topics.

Guide children who have chosen topics prompted by their own interests to surface bigger questions and important understandings. These may (or may not) be related to questions and understandings that have been the focus in the launching and guiding inquiries.

Essential Questions for Each Lesson

Revisit animal/environment EQs for students continuing to investigate related topics.

Through conferences, help all kids come up with big-picture questions for their own topics

Immerse	Investigate
Explore topics and questions	**Read, record new learning, and answer questions**
* Explore sources about a chosen topic or question. Help kids narrow their topic or refine their questions down to what's realistic to accomplish.	* Encourage kids to choose one or two questions about their topic and read with those questions in mind.
* Read online and print sources, study artifacts, mine experiences to build background knowledge in a topic or zero in on a question. Visit the library to gather a wide variety of sources.	* Kids choose how they will read, record new learning, and respond to it: in notebooks, with digital notes, on Post-its, and so on.
	Develop a line of questions
	* When kids investigate a topic, they may have several questions they want to answer. One question can lead to another.

become independent researchers. We encourage kids to use multiple sources. Part of becoming a researcher is learning to balance and integrate information from varying perspectives.

Resources

Tied to kids' interests, for example:

Books about endangered animals (sea turtles, elephants, manatees, and more)

Links to websites (review first)

Geode collection and field guide

Schedule library time to help kids find own resources

Coalesce

Choose a project to summarize and synthesize learning

* Review ways to pull together learning—self-published picture books, posters, field guides, brochures, and flyers.

Lesson: Summarize and Synthesize Information

* Guide kids to organize mind maps.

Confer about mind maps

* Coach kids in small groups and as they work independently to summarize and synthesize information.

Create picture books using a mentor text

* Encourage kids to record and illustrate their new learning through drawing and writing their own picture books.

Take Public

Share our work

* Let kids choose ways to present their work: displays, sharing sessions, informing others, and taking action.

* Remind kids about what they have learned about presenting their work. See "Teaching Kids How to Present Their Work," page 50.

Respond to others' work

Lesson: Respond to Others' Work

* Teach strategies for actively responding to each other's work.

Take action

* Kids are often moved to find ways to respond to the question "What can we do about this?" by finding ways to make a difference.

IMMERSE

■ Explore topics and questions

Some kids have already developed a passionate interest, drawn by the photograph of a stranded manatee, the sparkling crystals of a geode, or the plight of a sea turtle.

As kids come together to talk about what they want to investigate, William pipes up, "I really want to study manatees. I know that sometimes they get hit by boats while they are swimming. I wonder if that is why they are endangered. Why are boats near where they are swimming? Maybe I can find out." Several students discover a shared interest in endangered sea turtles and band together as a research team. We guide others, as yet uncommitted to a specific topic, to join a group or to continue general exploration to come up with a question or topic of interest to them. As kids read about their chosen topics, they wonder about new information, turning their wonderings into questions.

William reads as he explores the plight of manatees. Reading extensively prepares kids to ask their own authentic questions.

Kids teach the rest of the class how they came up with their research questions.

INVESTIGATE

■ Read, record new learning, and answer questions

Kids throw themselves into researching, taking notes on books about their topic, and consulting online resources. Artifacts and objects that kids discover and study also prompt questions and encourage further study.

VIDEO CLIP

Record important information and thinking.

Artifacts build intrigue and spark questions. Here kids investigate geodes and create a poster that explains their important attributes.

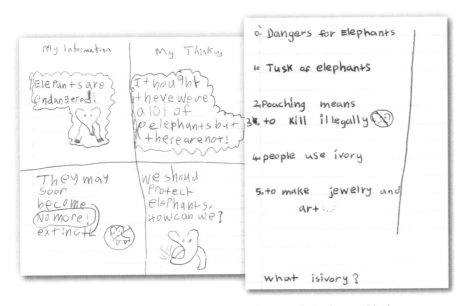

Mark finds a source that answers his questions about why elephants are endangered.

Intrigued by a class discussion about endangered elephants, Mark records his thinking in his journal and finds out about "dangers for elephants." He comments, "We should protect elephants. How can we?"

■ Develop a line of questions

A small group bursts with questions about sea turtles, which they have learned are endangered. They intently take notes (see below and the following page) covering the turtles' habitat loss, dangers from ocean pollution, and poaching, among other things. Their notes demonstrate the line of thinking each member of the group develops. Drawing and writing in this way allows each child to synthesize what they are learning independently. Later they will combine their learning, synthesizing it on a mind map.

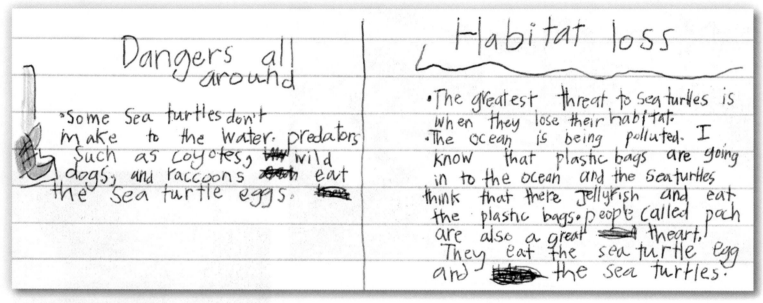

Information in kids' notes includes dangers that surround sea turtles, especially what happens to just-hatched turtles trying to reach the ocean. Kids note the problems that face sea turtles due to polluted oceans. As they draw and write information in notebooks, kids synthesize what they are learning in different ways.

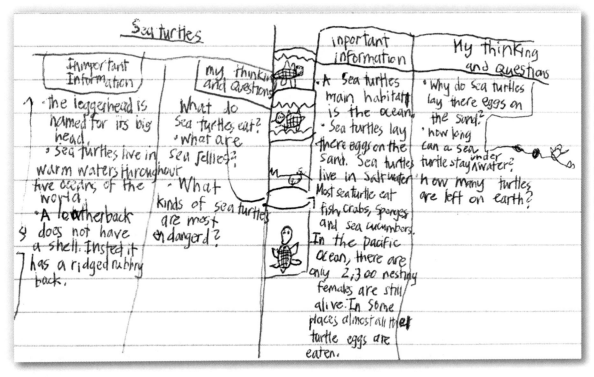

As this child takes notes on different kinds of sea turtles, she learns new information that raises the question: What kinds of sea turtles are most endangered? When she learns that nesting female turtles are not surviving and their eggs are being eaten, she has another question: How many turtles are left on earth?

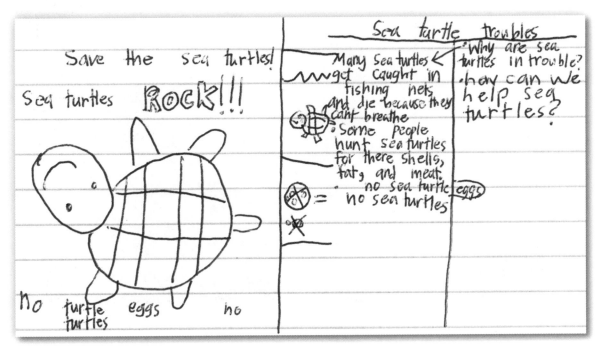

This child describes what happens when sea turtles get caught in fishing nets, or are hunted for their shells or meat. She is intent on saving sea turtles and wonders: How can we help them?

COALESCE

■ Choose a project to summarize and synthesize learning

See Lesson "Summarize and Synthesize Information," page 57

In writer's workshop, kids have learned different ways to present information. We review samples of the various forms they created—self-published picture books, digital texts, posters, brochures, and flyers (see "Reading and Writing in Support of Inquiry," pp. 109–74).

■ Guide kids to organize mind maps

A mind map provides a way to organize information graphically using "stems" to represent major categories of ideas around which kids can organize the information they have learned. To create the stems of the model mind map, we review our notes and identify two or three important ideas.

As they begin mapping, each big idea becomes one of the stems fanning out from the center where kids have written or illustrated their topic or question.

Using their notes on the previous page, kids create mind map stems for Habitat Loss, Dangers, and other facts about sea turtles.

■ Confer about mind maps

Conferences allow us to carefully target instruction to children's learning needs. A conference with the teacher allows a young researcher to talk through what he has done on his mind map about endangered elephants and what he is planning to write or draw next.

Brad Tell me about your mind map so far, Mark.

Mark (*Points to the gray stem*) This stem shows that they don't have a place to live because people are taking the land.

Brad You have illustrated and written about several ways that their land, or habitat, is disappearing. Tell me more about this stem.

Mark Sometimes people burn the land to build houses, then the elephants die in the fires. I drew an elephant and crossed it out, like I crossed out the trees when there was the fire.

Brad Wow, that is important information, and very unfortunate. Tell me about this part—where you wrote "grow crops."

Mark That's when people grow things to eat on the land, but when they do that the elephants can't live there anymore, so there is no place for them, and I crossed out the grasses.

Brad That sounds like people clear the land—so that is sort of the same thing. What will you draw or write about next?

Mark This stem is going to be about dangers to elephants—like hunters and people who kill elephants for their tusks.

Brad So thoughtful . . . I'll be eager to see your mind map when it's finished.

Creating stems for the mind map on endangered elephants.

■ Create and illustrate mind maps

Artistic representation requires kids to observe closely and create ways to show their learning using their imaginations. Together they plan out where to place information, then how to represent and draw specific ideas. The kids discuss options: "Let's make three stems: Habitat, Dangers, and Interesting Facts. How about if we color the habitat stem green to represent bamboo?"

Different colors represent different kinds of information. Here the group investigating manatees uses blue shading to represent clean ocean water. The students draw and write about polluted water on another stem, which they color red and gray, to symbolize how manatees' habitats are being threatened.

How to Help Manatees
1. Some people Rescew manatees. Thats are injured
2. They Released back
3. injured are Manatee
4. Many Conservation Organisatons.
5. you can help

Marina, working with William, records information about dangers that threaten manatees, including pollution and boats. She also begins to investigate how to help them.

■ **Create picture books using a mentor text**

Over and Under Picture Books

We encourage kids to use mentor texts as models when they create their own picture books. This child creates her own book based on the book *Over and Under*, which shows different habitats and environments above and below the water of a pond. See an example of a child's picture book about the Earth based on this mentor text on p. 108.

TAKE PUBLIC

Knowledge inspires action. Kids have chosen a variety of projects to summarize what they have learned. We also give them a choice of how to present their work—inviting classmates to view their displays, participating in sharing sessions, taking action to advocate for their issue. Kids not only respond orally after each presentation but also take some time to write Post-it reviews, complimenting or questioning each map, picture book, flyer, field guide, poster, and so on.

■ Share our work

When kids are ready to share their creations, they come together in a circle. This gives everyone an opportunity to see how unique each one is. The sea turtle group shares its mind map and engages in a conversation with the audience.

> "This is our mind map about sea turtles. We have three stems. One is about the dangers, one is about habitat loss, and another is about interesting facts. We colored it purple because it's dark at night—if the sea turtle eggs hatch at night, they may not make it to the ocean because they get eaten by raccoons or other animals. Also, the hatchlings think city lights are lights coming from the moon, and they follow it."
>
> "We colored some of it green to represent the ones that make it. On this stem we wrote about their predators and how people sell them. We told how some survive and some don't."
>
> "Another stem is pink—sea turtles are dying because the ocean is being polluted. Straws are a big threat. We think they try to eat them. Some sea turtles love jellyfish. They think the plastic bags we are throwing into the ocean are jellyfish and eat them."

When kids are ready to share their creations, they come together in a circle and share their mind maps. This gives everyone an opportunity to see how unique each one is.

"We are worried about sea turtles. What are some things we could do to save them? Turn and talk." (*Kids in the audience turn and talk and then share out.*)

"I saw that video of the sea turtle with the straw stuck in its nose. That is terrible!"

"Yes, we saw it, too. We went online and found a kid who went around to different restaurants near the beach and asked them to use paper straws, not plastic ones. And they did!"

■ Respond to others' work

See Lesson "Respond to Others' Work," page 58

After each researcher or group shares, they engage the class in a conversation about their work. They request:

"Does anyone have any questions, comments, or connections?"

"Please turn and talk about what you think about _____ and jot and draw on your Post-it."

"Who would like to share their thinking?"

Kids talk and write in response.

■ Take action

A picture book inspires action. Researchers investigating different species of sea turtles read the book *Follow the Moon Home.* In the story, kids in a seaside town successfully convince people living near the beach to turn off their lights at night so baby sea turtles that just hatched would crawl toward the ocean, not the illuminated houses. Landlocked students in the middle of Colorado went online to find out about their "own" sea turtle and why it was endangered. They created and shared posters, which were displayed in the hallway, about what they could do to help.

Researchers carefully read one another's mind maps and respond on Post-its.

Kids want to take action. A child shares information about green sea turtles and how to help them.

Addison uses the mentor text *Over and Under* to create her own book about the Earth.

Fossils can be plants or even elephants. They can be millions of years old.

You can find rocks everywhere. You live on rocks. Wherever you sit down you are sitting on rocks.

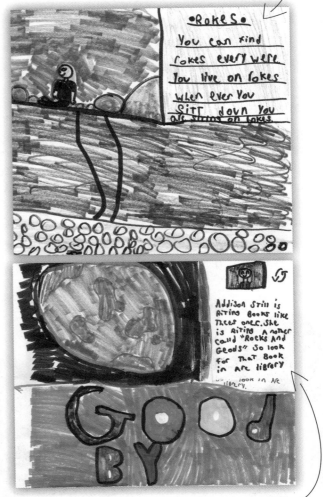

Minerals can be found in different places mostly caves. If you are looking for them look here.

Addison still is writing books like this one. She is writing another called "Rocks and Geodes." So look for that in our library.

Reading and Writing in Support of Inquiry

"Reading and writing are better when they are tools, not goals. . . . [They] are not about reading and writing in general. They are about reading and writing particular texts that are grounded in particular experiences."

—P. David Pearson

Much of what we ordinarily teach in reading and writing workshops transfers easily to the inquiry process. Kids use reading and writing in the service of learning about particular topics, whether introduced in researcher's workshop or in the reader's or writer's workshop.

The practices and lessons featured in this chapter are geared to helping kids read and write their way into and through the inquiry process. There's not time to do all the reading and writing lessons important to the research process in researcher's workshop, so we've included additional lessons here. You can adapt these lessons for large groups, small groups, or for individual conferences.

The Foundations of Reader's and Writer's Workshops

This book is grounded in the reading and writing workshop model. No other structure for literacy instruction gives readers the options that reader's and writer's workshop provide. With our support and guidance, readers choose just-right books and read extensively during workshop. Writers are given time to write to inform, understand, and learn. Teachers teach reading and writing strategies explicitly during lessons and conferences and kids share their learning and thinking at the end of the workshop, building community in the classroom.

Access

We stock our classrooms with plenty of books and resources, carefully curating the options and borrowing books from the school and public libraries, so that our collection is ever changing. School libraries, not to mention the school librarian, can make a huge difference in kids' reading lives. We have a rich selection of books in all genres accessible and available. It doesn't take much to get kids engaged in real or imaginary worlds: posters of sea creatures, picture books about dramatic events or compelling people, graphic novels, fantasy, mysteries, and adventure (Krashen, Lee, and Lao 2017). We constantly work to build our classroom libraries so kids have many compelling texts within reach.

Access to mentor texts in a variety of informational formats inspires writers to communicate their knowledge in rich and creative ways. Kids' use of appropriate formats (posters, picture books, field guides, digital texts, and so on) conveys information with imagination and accuracy.

Choice

We make sure that kids have time each and every day to lose themselves in books they choose, not just books that feed our curriculum. Kids need both. Kids have open-ended choice as well as what Allington calls "managed choice," when teachers guide kids' reading in classroom curriculum topics. When it comes to research, this prepares kids to take our inquiries into their own hands, exploring their own interests and answering their own questions.

Turning over the choice of writing topics and forms to the kids makes all the difference in their enthusiasm for writing. The focus becomes what kids want to express and share, not a choice someone has made for them. When kids are excited about research and investigation, they are eager to share their learning through writing, drawing, and making.

Time

It makes total sense: For kids to love to read—inside and outside the classroom—and to keep reading as they grow up, they need to spend a lot of time reading texts they can and want to read. Research on time kids spend reading is crystal clear: Allington (2002) reports that comprehension worksheets, test prep, and copying vocabulary get in the way of reading, sometimes resulting in only 10–15 minutes of actual reading in a 90-minute literacy block. So we're vigilant in making sure other activities don't get in the way of the time kids have to read.

The same goes for dedicating time for writing. We create predictable and consistent classroom routines. When kids write every day, the writing has forward momentum. Writers are creating, constructing, and composing, whether it's poetry, personal experience writing, or research.

Volume

Access + choice + time = volume. ACT now! A great acronym, and with ACT, volume soars (Harvey and Ward 2017). It's no secret—the more we read, the better we read. Kids' free, voluntary reading is the foundation on which they build to become readers for the rest of their lives. A large volume of high-success reading is the number one factor correlated with kids' reading progress/achievement (Krashen 2017; Allington 2012).

The writing principle is just like anything else we practice and learn to do well: The more kids write, the better they write. With opportunities to write in response to reading, math, science, social studies, or any other subjects, kids build writing fluency.

Response

Kids spend a lot of time responding to, talking about, and sharing books, one of the best ways for kids to become members of what Frank Smith calls "the literacy club" (1987). As kids read and respond in workshop, instruction happens during teacher–student conferences.

Ownership and Engagement

If kids are to become independent readers, taking ownership of and responsibility for their reading lives, they must relish what they read. In a classroom brimming with informational books, magazines, artwork, posters, photographs, and artifacts, not to mention online sources, kids soak up information and ideas enthusiastically.

When kids have choice in what and how they write, their ownership of and engagement with the writing process soars, and their voice rings true. Authentic writing and drawing about their experiences, new learning, and ideas comes from kids' desire to express themselves rather than from an orchestrated response. Voice, ownership, engagement, and enthusiasm are all integrally related.

> *"Voice is a driving force . . . it is the imprint of ourselves on writing."*
> —Donald Graves

Reading in Support of Inquiry

Building kids' independence and strategies as eager, curious readers can't help but carry over into their lives as explorers and researchers. In reader's as well as researcher's workshop, kids are chomping at the bit to learn more, ask questions, and dig deeper. To support kids' development as inquiring readers and researchers, we

- build independent reading habits
- teach comprehension strategies
- foster collaborative work and conversations.

We often introduce the practices and lessons you see here in reader's workshop and revisit them again (and again) in researcher's workshop. We suggest you interweave them with the core research lessons (pp. 48–57) depending upon your kids' intructional needs and the content you are teaching.

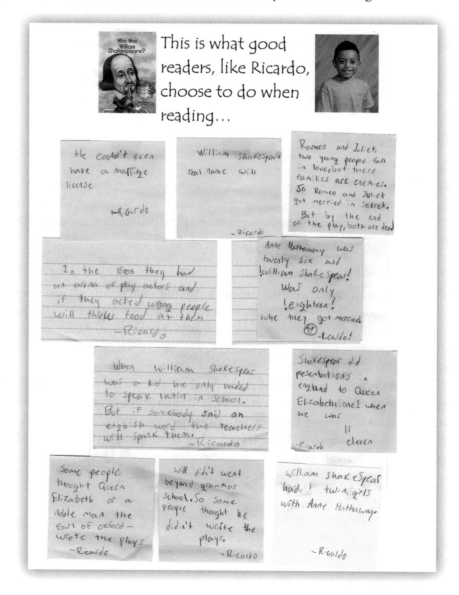

Build Independent Reading Habits

Like adults, kids have their own reading, viewing, and listening preferences. Some of us are news junkies, addicted to the online stream of information, an edgy blog, or the latest political book; others stay up half the night to finish a good mystery or novel; still others dive deep into poetry or song. Many of us do all of the above. As teachers, we honor kids' preferences yet at the same time we encourage them to broaden their choices, remembering Shelley Harwayne's advice that kids need to read "widely and wildly" (Harwayne 1999).

Here we share three practices with a lesson for each, introduced in reader's workshop early in the year. We then apply these same practices and lessons in researcher's workshop.

Practice	Why is this foundational to reader's workshop?	How is it applied in researcher's workshop?
Celebrate Reading *Lesson:* Share and Recommend Books	Seeking out and finding great reads energizes readers. Sharing these with others builds an enthusiastic community of readers.	Researchers are readers first and foremost. Sharing engaging resources, including books, websites, images and graphics, videos, and so on, builds excitement and intrigue.
Choice Reading *Lesson:* Choose a Good-Fit Book	Choosing their own books that reflect their reading preferences and interests builds kids' engagement and ownership.	Readers relish being in on the search. Kids can help to create "source sets," collecting topic-related resources and learning an important research skill—finding and evaluating resources.
Talk About Reading *Lesson:* Share a Book	"Understanding floats on a sea of talk" (after James Britton 1970). Teaching language frames for talking about books gets the conversation going.	Talk and discussion build content understanding. Responding to discoveries and new learning together builds collaboration and teamwork during the research process.

PRACTICE: Celebrate Reading

WHY

To energize and jump-start reading, on the first day we head straight to the library, sending the message that it's an extension of the classroom. Books are full of amazing information, and kids share intriguing, funny, or even mysterious reads. Recommending books to each other carries over to kids' inquiries and research: Kids seek out the dinosaur specialist who knows all about the most recent discoveries or the scientist who's an expert on the solar eclipse. Everyone's in on the search.

WHAT

Kids get upclose and personal with the library and the librarian to expand their knowledge about all the fun, exciting, potential reads out there. They revisit old favorites and explore new possibilities.

In the school or classroom library, we teach a simple routine:

- Browse the shelves, book bins, and so on, to find a favorite
- Peruse it, read it, reread it. Think about why it appeals to you. Enjoy it.
- Draw a picture that represents your book, jot down your thinking, and share it with others.

HOW

LESSON Share and Recommend Books

Purpose Kids broaden and deepen their reading diets by sharing great reads with others. Book recommendations happen all the time—both formally and informally. Here we create language that helps kids begin to make specific recommendations, which helps them get to know each other as readers.

Engage Kids race around the classroom or school library, gathering favorites and bringing them back to the circle on the rug. We hold these up—kids are already intrigued by their friends' choices.

Model/Guide "Here is a favorite of ours—it's a nature book. Let's make a poster to share it. We'll write the title, then we'll sketch what the book's mostly about, and add details. To recommend the book I'll add why I liked it and why you might like it, too."

Practice What kids do:

- Create a poster illustrating their book.
- Jot their recommendation right on the poster.
- Prepare to share these out with the whole class.

Share "This is what readers are always doing—sharing their reading and recommending books to their friends and family. Look at all the ways we described the books we are reading—they are funny, amazing, suspenseful. Some have tons of information. Notice we included graphic novels and wordless books! The sky's the limit!"

Take It Further Book posters are featured in a prominent place in the library, in the halls, in the classroom, in the front office. We put a pack of Post-its and a marker near the poster displays so kids can write their responses to the books and the poster creator on sticky notes and attach them to the posters.

PRACTICE: Choice Reading

WHY

Reading for a long period of time each day (in reader's workshop and throughout the day) builds self-suffiency, encourages self-regulation, and fosters enjoyment and engagement with books. When readers understand that there are many purposes for reading, they eagerly look forward to reading to learn, and research goes a lot more smoothly.

WHAT

Introduce a simple routine for independent reading: Choice Reading. To help kids choose books, we subscribe to Debbie Miller's ideas for teaching kids to choose what she calls "good fit" books (Miller 2013). Getting appropriate and intriguing books into kids' hands and helping them make thoughtful choices themselves are among our most important tasks as teachers. When kids have plenty of time to get immersed in their reading, whether it's during reader's workshop or researcher's workshop, they are more engaged with their books. No big surprise!

Kids learn a routine to:

- choose a good-fit book
- find a comfortable spot to work
- enjoy!

Kids find a comfortable spot for quiet concentration.

Reader's Workshop

We create a poster for expectations during quiet reading, so kids can remember and internalize what to do.

HOW

LESSON Choose a Good-Fit Book

Purpose Kids choose books they can and want to read. They think about these choices, considering how they read different books with different purposes in mind.

Engage Working with a small group, we ask kids to spend a few minutes choosing several books they think they'd like to read. We tell them we'll be talking about what makes a good-fit book and help them decide if their choices are a good fit (Miller 2013).

Model/Guide "Here are some questions I ask myself when I choose a book:

- Am I interested in this book?
- Can I read most of the words?
- Do I understand most of the ideas?
- Does it give me something to think and talk about?
- Do I enjoy reading it?

"Go ahead and look through the books you have selected. Let's think about these questions and sort them into two piles: 'a good fit' and 'not such a good fit.'

"I'm thinking this book looks too long, and it's not that interesting to me. I don't know a lot of the words. So I'll put it aside for now. Sometime I might pick it up again.

"This book looks challenging and I really am excited to find out about _____. I notice it has a lot of photographs and captions, so I will learn a lot from it. I'm going to give it a try, so I'll put it in my good-fit pile.

"This book is by an author I enjoy reading. I've read other books in this series and this is the latest one. I can hardly wait to get started!

"Now it's your turn. Think about each of the books you've selected. You're welcome to talk with each other as you sort your books. Then we'll share out our choices."

Practice Kids talk about their books, using the language we have just modeled.

Share As we share out book choices, kids learn to be more discerning about the books they choose to read. We discuss abandoning books—it's OK to put a book back that doesn't fulfill your expectations! We also discuss when we might want to tackle books that appear challenging at first, but that we can learn from, without having to read every word.

VIDEO CLIP

Share and talk about books.

PRACTICE: Talk About Reading

WHY

Simply talking about reading with a partner builds kids' understanding, engagement, and enthusiasm. Initially, kids talk together, informally sharing thoughts through turn-and-talks, think-pair-share, and so on. Over time, kids participate in more focused and structured conversations such as book clubs and study groups. As kids move into research, they talk about information they've unearthed and respond and react to one another's discoveries, often collaborating on projects. But it all begins with talk.

WHAT

We demonstrate sharing books with partners. Model actions and language for:

- sharing thinking, questions, opinions, reactions

- listening to and encouraging others to share; having a respectful conversation

- having fun and enjoying being part of the "literacy club."

Together with the kids, we create a chart of language for sharing. Conversational moves that encourage collaboration become part of kids' repertoire for talking about books.

HOW

LESSON Share a Book

Purpose Teach young readers specific language for talking about reading.

Engage "I can hardly wait to share my book with you all! I am reading _____, and it's all about _____. Notice how I talk about my book. Then you'll have a chance to share yours."

Model/Guide Kids sit in a circle with their books or in a comfortable spot with a small group or partner. We choose a volunteer to share her or his book so we can demonstrate a book conversation, sharing the language we use.

"Listen for a minute to our sharing conversation. Now it is your turn. Try it with the person sitting next to you. You can use some of the possible language for sharing a book from this chart. A polite way to begin is to say: '_____, would you please share your book with me?' And keep this in mind: The listener really has the biggest job, because when the reader finishes, the listener makes comments and asks questions to show they were interested in what the reader shared."

Possible Language for Sharing a Book

_____, would you please share your book with me?

As I was reading, I wondered . . .

I never knew about _____ until I read this book! I learned that _____.

One of the most interesting things I learned was _____.

I am reading _____. You might like this book because _____.

That's interesting . . . Say more about that . . .

Practice Kids think about what they just saw and try it with a partner.

Share As kids come back together, several pairs share out how they talked about their books.

Teach Comprehension Strategies

We don't teach strategies for strategies' sake—the purpose is always to give kids a toolbox of strategies to foster engagement, build knowledge, and enhance understanding. Comprehension and knowledge building are reciprocal. As students read with understanding, they create a store of knowledge that supports thinking and ongoing learning. This leads to thinking more deeply and critically, developing insight and empathy to understand the world and ourselves in relation to it. This happens as kids transfer foundational comprehension strategies to their own inquiries and investigations.

Here we share a few comprehension lessons for strategic reading in both reader's and researcher's workshop. For more, check out the Comprehension Toolkit series (Harvey and Goudvis 2016a, 2016b).

Practice	Why is this foundational to reader's workshop?	How is it applied in researcher's workshop?
Monitor Comprehension *Lesson:* Foster an Inner Conversation	Readers learn to pay attention to thinking as they read, listen, and view and to leave tracks of thinking through talking, writing, and drawing.	Researchers keep track of discoveries and new learning, reflecting on these and building a knowledge base about their topic.
Infer from Images and Features *Lesson:* Infer from Images	Deriving meaning from illustrations, photographs, and a variety of graphics adds to and deepens understanding of the text.	Graphic forms—photographs, diagrams, and the like—often carry a lot of information about a research topic. Discerning viewers interpret and learn content from many graphic forms.
Observe and Wonder About Real Stuff *Lesson:* Study and Learn from Artifacts	Objects and artifacts give kids experience with real things, add to their knowledge, and stretch their powers of observation. Viewing and seeing are important modes for learning.	Artifacts and objects can inspire inquiry and investigation and also encourage different ways of learning and responding (Lamb and Callison 2012).
Determine Importance When Reading Nonfiction *Lesson:* Analyze Information in an Infographic	Sorting information helps readers cull the most important details and note what is important to remember.	Effective research requires gathering information across several sources. Researchers synthesize information to share it and take it public.

When we use clear, explicit language to describe thinking and reading strategies, children learn to use this language in their responses and conversations. An ever-changing jargon of terms can confuse kids, so we teach strategies and the language that describes each consistently. A common language for comprehension encourages interactions and collaborations as kids read, write, talk, listen, view, and investigate. The following language frames are useful starting points for instruction:

MONITORING

My inner voice says _____.

The text makes me think _____.

This doesn't make sense _____.

Maybe if I read on, _____.

Huh? I don't get this part: _____.

Oh, now I get it.

I need to reread.

ACTIVATING AND CONNECTING

This reminds me of _____.

I noticed that _____.

I have a connection to my life: _____.

When this happened to me, _____.

I am surprised that _____.

I never knew that _____.

I can't believe that _____.

I used to think _____, but now I know _____.

I am amazed that _____!

That changes my mind.

QUESTIONING

I wonder _____.

I'm confused, I don't get this: _____.

What _____? Who _____?

How _____? Why _____?

My big question is _____.

I still wonder _____.

How come _____?

My lingering question is _____.

DETERMINING IMPORTANCE/SUMMARIZING AND SYNTHESIZING

I think this might be important: _____.

My opinion is _____, but the author is saying _____.

I think the big idea is _____.

I used to think _____, but now I _____.

The more important information seems to be _____.

I never realized that _____.

I think this part means _____.

Now I get it.

I think the message here is that _____.

In conclusion, _____.

A lingering question I have is _____.

INFERRING/VISUALIZING

I think that _____.

These clues tell me that _____.

I infer _____.

I have a picture in my mind _____.

I predict that _____.

The message here is _____.

Maybe it means _____.

The theme might be _____.

The words in the text _____ made me think _____.

These words created this image in my mind: _____.

The character's actions _____ made me think _____.

Based on what I already know, I think _____.

PRACTICE: Monitor Comprehension

WHY

"Reading is thinking" is our mantra. Monitoring is really a thinking disposition. Kids are always thinking as they read, listen, or view. We teach them to be aware of their thinking and use strategies to understand as they listen at first and then read on their own. Navigating a website app or viewing a video for information may require different strategies than opening up a book, so we teach strategies to fit the reading task at hand.

WHAT

We teach kids to monitor their thinking by first modeling our own questions, inferences, and connections. We share our inner conversation with the text so kids learn that they too should be listening to their inner voice as they read, listen, or view. During interactive read-alouds, we pause every few pages to stop and think ourselves, giving kids time to turn and talk. Then they jot and illustrate their thinking on Post-its, in journals, or on think sheets.

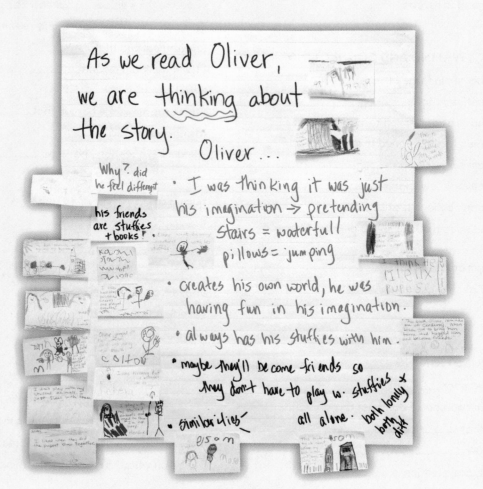

During an interactive read-aloud, kindergartners
share their thinking, which they record on Post-its.

HOW

LESSON Foster an Inner Conversation

Purpose To understand and make sense of text, readers need to listen to the voice in their head that speaks to them as they read. Helping kids become aware of and appreciate their own thinking as they read involves guiding them to write down and sketch their inner conversation.

Engage We bring kids up close and project an article or share a picture book, explaining that we will leave tracks of our inner conversation on Post-its or right on the page. We share ways to leave tracks of thinking using symbols for questions [?], inferences [I], background knowledge [BK], and new learning [L]. Kids create their own "codes" too.

Model/Guide "I'll think out loud, sharing the inner conversation I have as I read. I may have a question and write it down to see if I can answer it later. Or I might have a connection and say to myself, 'Hmm. That reminds me of _____.' I don't write down everything I am thinking, but leaving tracks of my inner conversation takes me deeper into my reading."

Practice Kids work together and continue reading the lesson text (or their own books or articles). They leave tracks of their thinking in the margins or on Post-its.

Share "Let's share some of the tracks of your thinking, your inner conversations. Notice how different our responses are—that's why talking about our reading is so interesting, we all think in different ways."

Take It Further Leaving tracks of thinking with codes and short responses is a pathway to writing short summaries, opinion pieces, or other forms of writing. When kids' "tracks" are in their own words, their voices shine through, and this leads to more authentic summaries of their learning.

PRACTICE: Infer from Images and Features

WHY

We've said it before: Meaning doesn't always arrive, fully dressed, on a platter. Reading the words or glancing at images is not enough. Kids glean lots of information from closely viewing images and features. We unpack and describe what it means to infer with the inferring equation: background knowledge + text clues = inference. With the plethora of visually elaborate websites, videos, and so on, researchers, especially, need lots of practice analyzing and learning from images and visual features.

WHAT

Kids find examples of images and features in magazines, books, and online and post these in the informational text nook. Kids work with a partner to infer and learn from various images, diagrams, maps, captions, and photos. As we share out each of these with the group, we discuss what the reader did to infer, which often results in new learning.

Kids give it a go, jotting inferences about images on Post-its.

HOW

LESSON Infer from Images

Purpose Use background knowledge to make inferences about photos and other visual features. Kids learn new information from viewing and inferring, transferring these strategies to their independent reading and viewing.

Engage "Let's view these images. Go ahead and turn and talk about what you notice in the images as well as your background knowledge. Remember our inferring equation: background knowledge + text clues = inference. That's right up here on the chart."

Model/Guide "Notice what I do as I view the image. I'll infer using my background knowledge, doing just what the equation says: We combine our background knowledge with text clues—in this case the image—to make an inference. We may also learn some new information from the image.

   "Go ahead and turn and talk with someone next to you about what you notice in the image and your inferences about it. Then we'll share out and you'll have a chance to try this with another image."

Practice Kids choose an image and work with a partner to jot down their inferences and what they learned from them.

Share Kids pop up right where they are working and quickly share their inferences and new learning. We display all our images up on a board with kids' Post-it responses for all to see.

Take It Further In a world with visuals bombarding kids 24-7, it's imperative for kids to sort and sift information and messages from images. After initially working with single images, photographs, and so on, kids tackle more sophisticated visual features: maps, diagrams, close-ups, cutaways, as well as collections of visuals on websites. Learning to screen out distracting visuals (such as pop-up ads) helps readers keep on track with their reading.

VIDEO CLIP

Observe, wonder, and learn about real stuff.

PRACTICE: Observe and Wonder About Real Stuff

WHY

What we can touch, feel, and experience enhances engagement. As researchers, kids "read" objects and artifacts, questions surface, and inferences abound. It takes practice to become a careful observer—what we call close viewing. Working with real stuff encourages careful observation and leads to further questions and exploration, research stategies all kids need to learn.

WHAT

Magnifying glasses, clipboards, and small notebooks are perfect for taking on field trips to encourage close viewing and observation. We share what scientists often do: take notes and create sketches to remember what they have seen firsthand. Observations involve both writing and illustrating. Careful observation leads to asking questions and doing research to answer them.

Kids create a museum in their classroom. They label artifacts and replicas as they prepare to host visiting classrooms to learn from their work.

HOW

LESSON Study and Learn from Artifacts

Purpose Nothing grabs kids' attention like the real thing (or an accurate replica). We create as many experiences as possible in and around the classroom for kids to observe and sketch, using evidence from artifacts like scientists do.

Engage "Let's take a look at these objects. What do you notice? What do you wonder? What do you infer? Scientists ask and answer these kinds of questions as they study artifacts. Turn and talk about what you see, notice, infer, and wonder."

Model/Guide "I'm looking at _____. I'm inferring that _____. I notice some details here. I have a question. I wonder _____. I'll draw and write my observations in my notebook."

Practice Kids set up a journal with space for both drawing and writing. Sometimes they can draw objects more accurately and completely than they can describe them in words, but we encourage both.

Share We ask kids to turn and share with a small group so that they have more in-depth conversations about their observations and questions.

Take It Further Create a Discovery Center—once kids find out more about their artifacts, they can create labels and captions describing these and become curators of a museum display (see pp. 8–11 in "Creating a Culture for Inquiry").

PRACTICE: Determine Importance When Reading Nonfiction

WHY

Kids are barraged with information, images, text, pop-up boxes, and links all day and every day. They have to sort and sift all the information that comes at them, so determining what's important to learn and remember from different sources is essential.

WHAT

Infographics are complex combinations of text and visuals that appeal to young readers but that require careful reading. Kids use strategies to determine what's important by paying close attention to a plethora of features, analyzing minimal text, and interpreting images. They surface important information and use a variety of response formats to help them sort and organize facts and ideas. We create a chart of questions to consider as kids read and view infographics.

Kids ask questions about and make sense of an infographic.

HOW

LESSON Analyze Information in an Infographic

Purpose Getting to what's important depends on our purpose for reading. Reading to learn important information means we sort out what's most significant from less important but often salient details. In infographics, writers and illustrators use both words and images to share important information. Helping readers determine what is most important about the infographic is at the core of this lesson.

Engage "Take a look at this infographic! Let's think for a minute and then talk about what it is about—what is it trying to teach us? Notice the images and features as well as the words. We will use this chart to guide us to analyze the infographic."

Model/Guide "Always read the title first. This infographic is called _____. Let's see, what is it about?" (*We discuss.*) "Now let's look closely at the images. Here I see a diagram of _____. It helps to read the labels and the bold print. Sometimes the features show movement; arrows do that. What do we learn from the images?" (*We discuss.*) "It also helps to ask questions while we view it. Hmm, I'm wondering: What's that?

"Let's read the text here. Turn and talk about what you think is most important." (*We discuss.*)

Analyzing an Infographic	
Name the topic of the infographic.	What is the infographic about? What are the big ideas?
View the graphic features. Read the text.	What do we learn from the text? What do we learn from the features? Images? How do the words and graphics work together?
Jot down your questions.	What questions do you have about the information and ideas? What would you like to know more about?
Determine the message.	How would you summarize the important information? What is the overall message of this infographic?

Practice Kids continue to analyze the infographic, using the questions on the chart.

Share We wrap up with kids sharing the important information or message they learned from analyzing the infographic.

Take It Further Kids analyze and interpret other texts and visuals including websites, diagrams, maps, and others to determine what is most important to remember.

Foster Collaborative Conversations

In this hurried life that all of us lead, we seldom gather every night around the dinner table to engage in conversation. Or when we do, our phones or media events might be competing with the conversation. The best way to learn how to have a conversation is simply to have one, but not everyone is a natural conversationalist. So we'd better start teaching the art of conversation in school. Collaborative conversations revolve around rich talk about books, articles, ideas, and everyday experiences. They are a natural extension of what has been happening in young people's lives. Participating in reader's workshop, using the comprehension strategies kids have under their belts, results in more substantive conversations inside and outside of school. Teaching kids to ask questions, make inferences, connect to experiences, and synthesize big ideas leads to a fuller richer life.

Collaborative conversations enhance engagement, understanding, and insight. Fielding and Pearson (1994) capture the essence of why we give kids opportunities—and teach them how—to participate in many different kinds of discussions and conversations about their reading each and every day.

Here are practices that foster group conversation and discussion in both reader's and researcher's workshops:

Practice	Why is this foundational to reader's workshop?	How is it applied in researcher's workshop?
Engage in the Art of Conversation *Lesson:* Model a Collaborative Conversation	Sharing thinking, expressing opinions, and building on each other's ideas in small-group conversations shares group knowledge and inspires new ideas.	Throughout investigation, coalescing, and taking public, kids profit from talking together to build knowledge, summarize and synthesize their learning, and share their work with others.
Participate in a Study Group *Lesson:* Learn Study Group Routines	Collaborative strategies—taught using language frames and routines—build comprehension and help kids navigate discussions.	Study groups provide a setting for collaborative research. Kids who know how to work together boost each other's learning and invent pathways for further research.
Dig Deeper in a Picture Book Group *Lesson:* Discuss Picture Books	Discussions of ideas and themes in books foster understanding and insight.	Through shared reading, kids build collective knowledge about content or the research topic, discussing ideas, themes, and different perspectives.

"*Conversation . . . gives students another opportunity to practice and build comprehension skills collaboratively, build[ing] the all-important community of readers.*"
—Linda Fielding
and P. David Pearson

PRACTICE: Engage in the Art of Conversation

WHY

Conversational give-and-take in a classroom—kids giving each other information, enhancing one another's ideas, challenging one another's opinions—geometrically increases the breadth and depth of learning. Many brains thinking are greater than one. Not all kids find it easy to participate, even in small groups. But all kids do benefit from explicit models and guided opportunities to talk together.

WHAT

We provide kids with a structure and specific language to get them started. In the following lesson, kids get the big picture of a collaborative conversation by watching one happen. Kids see classmates and their teacher demonstrate the following.

We meet with a couple of kids ahead of time and plan out what we will discuss, choosing a topic of interest to the kids in the fishbowl. We show them how to listen carefully to one another, use collaborative language, and talk about questions and thoughts. This bird's-eye view of the process helps kids see a conversation unfold over time so they have a vision of what's possible.

The Art of Conversation

- Stop and talk.
- Engage in thoughtful conversation.
- Use the language of comprehension to share responses.
- Use respectful and encouraging language to get everyone talking and participating.
- No need to raise hands; start talking when someone else stops.
- Have fun sharing ideas about and enthusiasm for books, ideas, and experiences.

Kids share their ideas and enthusiasm for books.

LESSON Model a Collaborative Conversation

Purpose What does a collaborative conversation look and sound like? To show kids a conversation in action, the class sits in a circle around the teacher and two kids demonstrate how to talk about books, ideas, and experiences. Kids observe the process and discuss what they notice participants saying and doing.

Engage "We're going to show you what a collaborative conversation looks like. The three of us will be talking about a topic we are all interested in. Your job is to watch carefully what we do and what we say. In a few minutes we'll ask you to share what you noticed us doing and saying."

Model/Guide "Let's have a conversation about _____. As I thought about this, I had a connection that I'd like to share." (*Shares the connection.*) "Did this topic remind you of anything?" (*Kids share a connection if they had one.*) "I also had this question: _____? Any thoughts about that?"

   The small group continues to talk respectfully for three or four minutes. Turning to the rest of the group, "Now it's your turn to tell us what you noticed us doing and saying during our conversation. What did you notice us saying and doing?" (*Kids share out observations.*) We create a chart with language stems and conversational moves to guide kids.

What We Say	What We Do
This was really interesting . . . I was a little confused . . . I was amazed . . .	Listen. Look at the person while he or she is talking.
I had a question. I made an inference . . . I made a connection . . . I never knew . . .	Take turns talking. Make eye contact.
What are you thinking, _____? What are you wondering, _____?	Make sure everyone participates.
I agree . . . I had a different idea . . . I beg to differ. I was thinking . . .	Feel free to agree or disagree in a respectful way.

Practice On subsequent days, we review the chart we created and set up opportunities for kids to apply the guidelines to their own conversations—about books, about topics they are researching, about collaborative projects they are working on.

PRACTICE: Participate in a Study Group

WHY

If small-group discussions are going to be effective, kids must take turns and listen carefully to other group members, be ready to participate fully in the group's task or activity, and learn to be aware of and reflect on their own participation and how the group functions as a whole. A tall order, as group discussion skills take a lot of practice and effort (Harvey and Daniels 2015).

WHAT

Kids build their knowledge through talk and discussion, all day every day. They get together in study groups to investigate a topic they are interested in, which is exactly what happens during researcher's workshop. Curricular investigations and the nonfiction reading that supports them provide the perfect opportunity for instructional conversations around new learning. We teach conversational frames for discussing information, recording and keeping track of new learning, and making group decisions about what to do next.

During reader's workshop as most of the class reads independently, we pull a small group to form a study group. Teaching study group routines in small groups allows us to provide undivided attention as kids get started.

HOW

LESSON Learn Study Group Routines

Purpose Working together energizes kids to learn and share what they are learning. We work with a small group to give them the tools, procedures, and language to build knowledge collaboratively.

Engage Kids are excited to talk about what they are learning and wondering. We introduce the chart of language kids can use to make their study group run smoothly.

Model/Guide "In your study group, you'll want to do the following:
  o Talk about your questions and the information you're gathering.
  o Record/jot down your new learning.
  o Sum up your learning by talking about it.
  o Decide what your group will read and study next.

"Here are some ideas for language to use during your discussions. You can refer to this chart as your group meets together."

Study Group Conversation

To talk about your questions and the information, you might say:
  The question I really want to find out about is _____.
  I'm really interested in _____.
  I used to think _____, but now I know _____.
  This is amazing. I never knew _____.

To encourage discussion in your group, you might say:
  What are you interested in learning about, _____?
  _____ [name], what questions do you have about _____?

To talk about how to record new learning, you might say:
  Let's each write down what we learn in our notebooks.
  I'm going to add a sketch to my information right here.
  After we read and write, let's share with each other what we found out.

To sum up learning/decide where to go next, you might say:
  So today I learned _____. What did you find out, _____?
  That's interesting. We learned different things about _____.

Practice and Share Kids try it, report back on how the group process went, and discuss how their research will move forward.

PRACTICE: Dig Deeper in a Picture Book Group

WHY

Thought-provoking picture books raise questions and tackle issues through compelling narratives. Small groups read books that speak to the essential questions and enduring understandings under study so kids can consider big ideas and gain a multifaceted view of a topic.

WHAT

Reading a variety of picture books builds kids' interest and intrigue as we launch a topic study or inquiry. Gathering historical fiction, trade books, realistic fiction, even primary sources such as journals and diaries, offers kids a wide variety of options for building their knowledge. Kids read books with a small group, keeping essential questions in mind. Conversations and discussions about ideas and themes surface in different texts so that when kids share with others, they build their collective knowledge about the topic.

Kids build background knowledge about a topic as they engage in picture book conversation.

Kids pass picture books around the circle and choose one to read with a partner.

HOW

LESSON Discuss Picture Books

Purpose To build background knowledge and intrigue about a topic kids are investigating, tying new learning to essential questions.

Engage "Check out all these different books! We're going to do a quick book pass—spending just a few minutes perusing a book and then passing it on to the person sitting next to you in the circle. After you've explored several books, you can look more closely at all the possibilities and then choose one you want to begin reading with your book group.

"All of these books relate to our topic. Let's review our essential questions and enduring understandings, because we want to keep these in mind as we read. These books represent many different perspectives, so we'll get what we call a multifaceted view of this topic through our reading and book group discussions."

Model/Guide "I'll show you how I think about this book as I begin reading it and looking through it. I'll consider . . .

- Who's telling the story? What's the point of view?
- What's the book's genre? Historical fiction? Realistic fiction? Nonfiction? Is it a primary source like a diary or journal? Why is it important to read a variety of genres when we are learning about a topic?
- Are different perspectives expressed in this one book? If so, what are they?"

Practice After kids have read and talked about their books, they consider these questions:

- What did you learn about our essential questions and enduring understandings from reading this book?
- What big ideas and themes did you glean from this book and your conversations about it?
- What lingering questions does the book suggest for your group? For our class to consider as we continue to study this topic?

Share Kids who read each book post their responses to the questions, and the class as a whole discusses a visual way to synthesize learning across texts.

Writing in Support of Inquiry

> *The classroom hums with activity: Two kids create a mural of a rain forest habitat, discussing whether toucans live in the canopy or the emergent layer, or both. Another child writes a caption about a jaguar crouched in the understory, lurking near a stream, lying in wait for its dinner. Consulting the Yosemite website, another pair creates a summary response about John Muir, marveling that during his life he walked 1,000 miles and later was one of the first people to scramble up Half Dome. Writing a field guide page about geodes, one child answers her question, "How do the crystals get inside a plain old rock?"*
>
> *Down the hall in the library, the librarian helps a child add a pop-up praying mantis to his poster on insect hunters, writing in vivid detail about its ferocious eating habits. Kids listening in are mesmerized, getting ideas for their own interactive design techniques. This isn't your typical "just the facts" nonfiction. Kids are encouraged to express their unique voices, imaginative flair and original ideas.*

"Writing in Support of Inquiry" focuses on how kids learn to write and draw informational text of all kinds. Early in the year, they learn basic routines for writing in both writer's and researcher's workshops. Different formats allow kids to express their purposes for writing nonfiction. Workshops encompass all

sorts of writing formats: teaching books, self-published picture books, digital books and presentations, posters, brochures. Kids' imaginations and original thinking are expressed through art and illustration, the creative use of graphics and design techniques that capture the reader's attention and interest.

Two instructional principles underlie these writing practices:

1. Writing and illustrating are parallel composing processes, each building on the other. As kids make decisions about what they write and draw, they build ideas and construct meaning in different ways. They envision what they want to say or share, and writing and drawing are acts of expressing this vision—whether they are putting pen and marker to paper or composing and illustrating on a digital device.

2. Mentor texts are essential teaching tools that open up many possibilities for creating nonfiction as kids write across the day—in writer's and researcher's workshops. Examples include magazine articles, online resources and websites, field guides, brochures, infographics, poetry, and songs. We choose mentor texts for design and structure as well as the writing itself.

To support writing to learn and inform in our workshops, we

- establish writing routines
- build a repertoire of formats
- incorporate design elements.

> *"Once students learn to read as writers, every act of reading has the potential to deepen their understanding of the craft of writing, too."*
> —Katie Wood Ray

Establish Writing Routines

A predictable writing workshop each day sets the tone for an intellectually rich environment where students can thrive as writers. Kids develop writing strategies and techniques in the context of real writing. Routines comprise a flexible set of steps that can be used for writing in different genres and for many different purposes. These practices may be launched in writer's workshop initially, but are transferred to kids' writing in the researcher's workshop.

Here we share how these practices happen in both:

Practice	Why is this foundational to writer's workshop?	How is it applied in researcher's workshop?
Write from Experience *Lesson:* Start Writing	The understanding that "what we can talk about, we can write and draw" helps kids put thoughts, ideas, questions, and experiences into writing and illustrations.	Writing is exploration and making sense of what we find out. Kids can't resist sharing quirky details, questions, or startling facts through talking, writing, and drawing.
Use Vivid Language and Imagery *Lesson:* "Show Not Tell" in Writing	Poetry, picture books, and magazines are mentor texts where kids can find sensory details and descriptive language to give a lift to their own writing.	We prepare kids to "show not tell" as they compose informational text. We collect and share models of powerful description from magazine articles, online sources, and image-laden texts.
Record Observations, Experiences, and Thinking *Lesson:* Record Observations in Field Notes	Kids "notice, pay attention, marvel and [are] fascinated with the world around them" (Harwayne 2001). We share journals, poetry, and sketch books as mentor texts showing kids ways to write "in the moment."	For kids who are accustomed to writing about their own interests and experiences, reading the field notes and journals of practicing scientists or historians inspires them to write to investigate their passions.
Respond to Each Other's Writing *Lesson:* Give and Get Feedback	Seeing their work through a reader's or viewer's eyes is writers' first step toward learning to revise: to clarify and improve writing.	Researchers change and revise thinking and writing in the face of new information, getting input and ideas from other researchers.

Oct 22 all

Sully, Anders, Dylan

Sully, Dyley Anders,
Thank you
for teaching
us about
frogs. Love,
Bnd

The poison-dart frog. And more!

the poison-dart frog is endangerd!

there are many different kinds of poison-dart frogs.

Poeple think that poison dart frogs are dangerous but they are just trying to protect themselfs from getting killed **so dont harm them!**

please dont hurt me!

Some poison-dart frogs have spots and Some have blobs.

Did you know poison-dart frog come in menny colers Like thes blow, pink I will do in exsample in colers

questions from the kids:

poison-dart frogs have poison on there backs

poisen

the poison-dart colors are: blue, red, orange, purple, yellow, black, and green and pink and turciouse.

The poison-dart frog has a chance of going to extinction 92 percent

Help me!

poison-dart frogs sqeuze poison out of there bodys.

sqeeeeeeeeBeeuze!

questions: ly the creators were do poison-dart frogs live?

poison

eye   head

feet

feet

PRACTICE: Write from Experience

WHY

Kids have lots of ideas to write about. We listen in on their conversations throughout the day. When we do, we hear their ideas for writing in their talk. They are constantly sharing stories of something that they recently did or observed, although they may not recognize these experiences as ideas for writing. What do we do? We honor their ideas and encourage kids to write them down.

WHAT

As the class is walking to music, listen. On the way to lunch or art, listen. Talking about our experiences helps us write. This is how we build excitement for writing workshop, and kids have yet to pick up a pen!

We begin the workshop by doing what we ask kids to do: by writing. We model the broadest range of possibilities—what we think, observe, and experience—and show kids how we jot our ideas down.

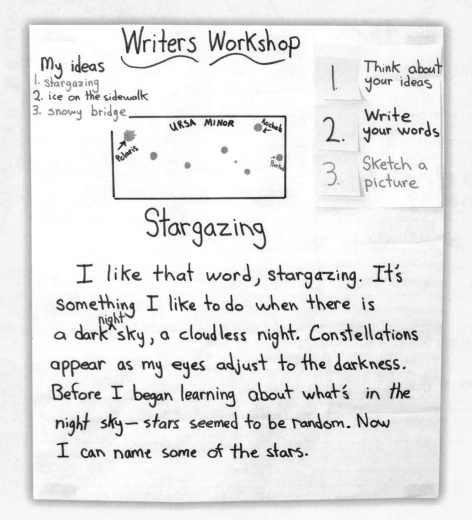

LESSON Start Writing

Purpose To capture ideas, talk about them, and begin writing.

Engage We talk with kids about possible ideas they can write about. For starters, we ask them to turn and talk about an experience they would like to share with someone sitting near them. We point out that when we talk about our experiences, it's easy to take the next step and write them down. Kids share out some of what they talked about and we celebrate these as experiences they can write down.

Model/Guide We think aloud about three experiences we could write about and list these on a chart.

"I am going to tell you about some experiences I would like to write about. One night I looked up at the sky and noted that it was dark and filled with stars. I'll call this *stargazing*. Another idea came to me one day when it had snowed a lot and the sidewalk was very slippery. And another idea came to me as I rode across a really snowy bridge on my bike. I'll list these three ideas on our chart.

"Notice that I am writing about something I know about and care about. I'm choosing an idea and I am writing to explore it. I think I'll choose stargazing to write about. There's a picture in my mind I want to sketch, so I'll do that, too."

Next we jot the process that kids will follow on the chart and ask who is ready to try it. If kids find it hard to come up with an idea, we confer with them and prompt them to tell us an idea. Then we encourage them to write down just what they said.

> When we write, we
>
> - think about our ideas
> - write our words
> - sketch a picture.

Practice Kids get their notebooks and have a go. As they begin to settle in and write, teacher–student conferences help them get started and nudge them to keep going. We often ask kids to tell us their idea and then say it back to them as they write down the words.

Share We come back together to share our writing, sitting in a circle so everyone can see and hear as kids read their writing and show their illustrations. There's often laughter, excitement, and eagerness to share—the beginning of a community of writers.

PRACTICE: Use Vivid Language and Imagery

WHY

"Authentic nonfiction paints pictures with words and [creates] a visual image of [what] the text is saying in the mind's eye" (Harvey 1998, 158). Writers, above all, want to communicate information and make it come alive for readers. They show rather than simply tell. Kids learn about the difference between "just the facts" writing and writing that uses vivid language by reading and noticing the differences first.

WHAT

We can share writing from an encyclopedia or other dull text to illustrate boring, lifeless facts. Kids can search a variety of well-written trade books for descriptive language that shows rather than tells and collect these as examples to use in their own writing. Once they note these distinctions, they are ready to have a go at writing with rich, vivid language themselves.

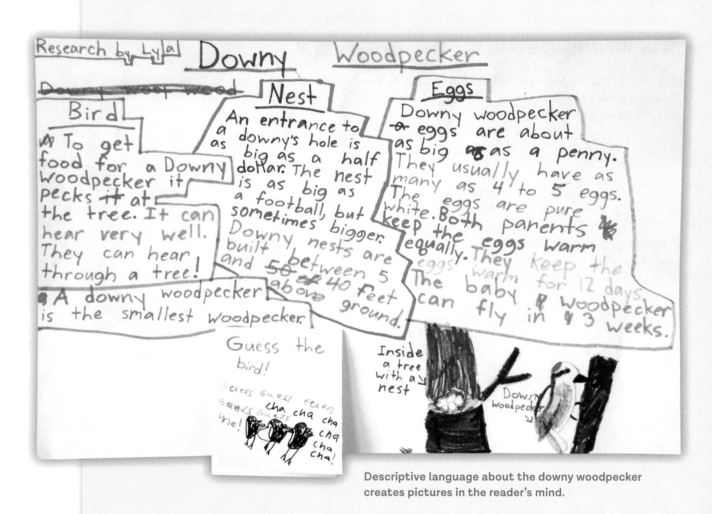

Descriptive language about the downy woodpecker creates pictures in the reader's mind.

HOW

LESSON "Show Not Tell" in Writing

Purpose To pump up writing with vivid, descriptive language that creates a visual picture in the reader's mind. Articulating how sensory details and rich description create specific images supports kids to "show not tell."

Engage Kids peruse a variety of nonfiction trade books, which includes straightforward informational writing and writing filled with imagery and vivid description. We notice and share

- descriptive words that paint a picture in our minds
- words that show action—like a movie in our head.

Model/Guide "Let's try writing with vivid language. We can describe what's happening in this photograph: You can see a polar bear waiting by a hole in the ice. From my background knowledge, I'm thinking he is waiting to catch a seal to eat.

"Watch while I write:

> Waiting, waiting, waiting. The polar bear crouches by a hole in the ice. He knows a seal may come up to breathe air and he wants to catch it to eat it. Suddenly, the water splashes and a dark nose with whiskers pops out of the water. Pounce!

"I'll read it once more and then we'll share out words that painted a picture in our minds.

"Who noticed some words that have a lot of action, words that describe what is happening here?"

Bryan The dark nose popped out of the water.

Aimee *Pounce*. The polar bear pounced on the seal to catch it.

Teacher Tell us more about the picture in your mind, Aimee.

Aimee He jumped on the seal—so I think the polar bear probably jumped right in the water to get the seal.

"That's quite a description! Who else can see that happening? Who else has a mind picture of what is happening here that we could describe? Let's brainstorm a few more ideas."

Together, the group comes up with other actions—the polar bear swiping at the seal, the seal spinning and gliding through the water to escape—and we jot these down.

Practice Kids, using their background knowledge and beginning with some of the phrases we've recorded on the chart, try writing and their own versions of the scene.

Share Kids come back to share and talk about their vivid descriptions.

Use observations and websites to create field notes.

PRACTICE: Record Observations, Experiences, and Thinking

WHY

Participating in an inquiry always involves gathering information. In addition to noting information from print sources, digital or traditional, researchers write to describe or explain an observation or experience. Recording learning from video or real-time observations, made possible in a 24-7 digital world, requires care and accuracy and often leads to questions for further investigation. Drawing or sketching allows us to record aspects of what we see or experience that cannot be captured in words.

WHAT

Kids collect and record their experiences, real or virtual, with accuracy by writing and sketching, jotting down their thinking and questions in field notes, a science notebook, a reading log, a journal, a lesson book, or another means of recording learning. Kids write to learn using a variety of note-taking scaffolds, for example: Notes and Sketches/Thinking and Questions; Important Information/My Thinking; or Observations/Thinking and Questions. Mentor texts include journals, collections of photographs, notebooks, and field notes from anthropologists, ornithologists, historians, and others.

These field notes were written as a child observed several birds via a webcam. She responds to her observations with questions and inferences, just as scientists do.

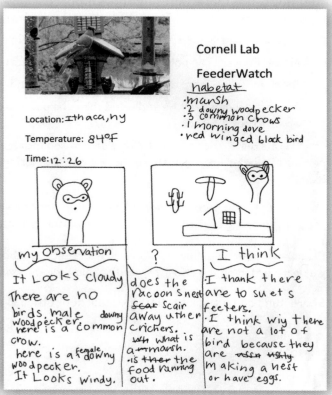

HOW

VIDEO CLIP

Watch a child teach how to record field notes.

LESSON   Record Observations in Field Notes

Purpose Kids use mentor texts to notice and emulate how researchers of all stripes keep track of their observations, experiences, and questions. Kids' descriptions and explanations need to be accurate and include important details. The researcher's thinking and questions are equally important as fodder for further investigation.

Engage We share various ways (writing and drawing) of recording observations and learning from experiences. John J. Audubon's notebooks, Jane Goodall's field notes, and Snowflake Bentley's photographs are all examples of ways that keen observers and researchers keep careful track of what they are learning and studying.

Model/Guide "Let's take a look at this webcam as it records what is actually happening. Watching this real-time video I can jot my observations in my two-column field notes."

Observations	Thinking and Questions

"I'll write what I observe in the Observations column in my field notes. I can also make a quick sketch. This new information may prompt some questions, so I'll write those in the Thinking/Questions column.

"It's tough to write everything we observe or hear, so let's think about what is most important. Then I'll add what I think about the information in the Thinking column.

"I'm going to sketch my observations and I'll be careful to accurately draw what I see."

Practice We give kids other texts, images, or videos on the topic of our inquiry for them to carefully observe and take notes on.

Share Kids share out what they learned from their various observations.

Take It Further Kids use these strategies for recording accurately and describing information for their own research topics.

PRACTICE: Respond to Each Other's Writing

WHY

To build kids' confidence, they share their writing and ask, "Does anyone have any questions, comments, or suggestions?" This question opens the door to readers' honest reactions and responses, and the writer gleans suggestions from her or his audience. Kids often listen to suggestions and add to their writing while it's fresh in their mind and they are motivated. We remember to emphasize being respectful and encouraging as we do this, just like a real editor.

WHAT

Teaching kids respectful conversational moves and language for giving and getting feedback on their writing happens as soon as kids are ready to share what they have written with others.

Lola's drafting and revision process

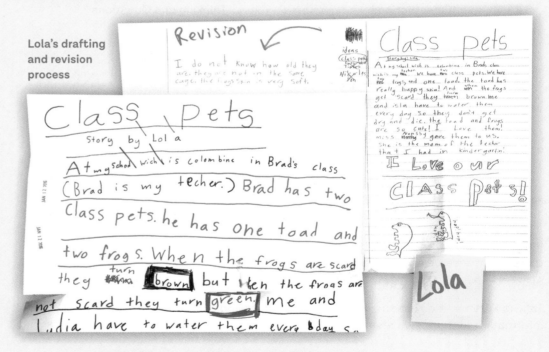

This child responds to written comments from her peers about her piece "The Dead Finch."

HOW

LESSON Give and Get Feedback

Purpose To get a dialogue going about writing. Kids learn a routine for sharing and asking for suggestions and questions. They listen to readers' feedback and possibly add to or revise their writing accordingly.

Engage "Here's what we'll do now that we have written about our experiences. We want to hear each other's questions and suggestions as we share our pieces."

Model/Guide "Here is a chart of how we can talk about our writing. These are questions and comments we can ask a writer. Sometimes we want to better understand what the writer is trying to say, so we ask a question. Or we may have an idea for something the writer can add to his or her piece, so we respectfully make a suggestion. And sometimes we just want a little more information, so we ask the writer to tell us more."

Feedback Chart

I had a question about _____.

I wondered . . .

I have a suggestion . . .

Could you tell me more about _____?

"Let's try it. Here is my piece about stargazing (see p. 142). I'll read it to you again."

" I like that word *stargazing*. It's something I like to do when there is a dark night sky, a cloudless night. Constellations appear as my eyes adjust to the darkness. Before I began learning about what's in the night sky, stars seemed to be random. Now I can name some of the stars."

"Does anyone have any questions or suggestions for me?"

Jaime I have a question. Did you see any meteors?

"Actually, Jaime, I did, and it was a blue-white streak that I saw for just a moment and then it disappeared. I'll add that to my piece. Thanks for your question, which gave me a good idea for adding to my piece!"

Practice "Go ahead and find a partner. Remember: Listen to your partner read his or her piece, talk together, and don't forget to use the language on the chart as you respond. Be sure you each have time to share and talk about your pieces."

Share Partners come to the circle to share out what they did as they talked about and responded to each other's writing.

Build a Repertoire of Formats

"When kids express themselves in writing, they gain a sense of audience, agency, and purpose."

—Donald Graves

Kids (and the rest of us) write for many different purposes. Teaching young writers a repertoire of formats for writing gives them many choices and options. What inspires one writer one day may not the next day. A kid who is less than enthusiastic about writing a paragraph might eagerly embrace making an infographic or a poster.

We teach these (and other) formats for kids to communicate in both writer's and researcher's workshops:

Practice	Why is this foundational to writer's workshop?	How is it applied in researcher's workshop?
Explore a Variety of Writing Formats *Lesson:* Explore Different Formats and Purposes	Learning about the many reasons we write, seeing examples, and experimenting with different formats encourages kids to explore new ways to express themselves.	As they summarize, synthesize, and present their research findings, kids explore and imagine a variety of nonfiction formats for writing/drawing to learn and teach content. They match the format to the purpose for writing.
Share Expertise and Guide Experiences *Lesson:* Create a Field Guide	Studying and collecting different kinds of instructional texts helps kids understand their different purposes.	Taking research public often involves teaching a reader or viewer what the researcher has learned. Kids think about and adjust their writing and graphics to engage and inform their audience.
Distill Information for Easy Access *Lesson:* Create a Brochure or Pamphlet	Writing to retell events, give directions, provide advice, and so on prepares kids to present information clearly with text and images.	Writing to inform and teach others is a real-world skill—especially when writers need to make the information succinct and engaging to their audience.
Organize in Sequential Order *Lesson:* Make a Time Line	Relating events in sequential order makes sense of the events and reveals an understanding of what happened and when it happened.	Explanations in science or history often involve recounting events, steps in a process, and so forth in a linear, sequential order.
Write to Persuade *Lesson:* Write a Persuasive Letter	Practice writing personal experiences, letters, editorials, and placards with a clear point of view is a foundation for persuasive writing.	Effective persuasion through letters, essays, and speeches weaves in thoughtful facts and evidence gleaned from research.

Kids created brochures after a field trip to the National Center for Atmospheric Research.

NCAR

We made a Bubble By Puting in hot Water. The Bubble expand.

This is the lightning tub

This is the Tornato

VIDEO CLIP

▶

Explore and share
ways to write
to inform.

PRACTICE: Explore a Variety of Writing Formats

WHY

To help kids become aware that there is a big world of nonfiction out there, some of which is already familiar to them, we collect mentor texts. Kids bring in newspapers, letters, notes, postcards, brochures, pamphlets, magazines, books, articles, emails, illustrations, and photographs. Together we create a writing nook that displays these forms. Over time, we add to this display, imagining new and different ways of expressing ourselves.

WHAT

As kids bring in different forms of writing, they are responsible for sharing with the group and writing a short caption to describe it. We also start our message board as a form of communication. Other possibilities include a postcard nook for written correspondence. In the discovery center, there are stacks of Post-its to capture kids' questions and new information about the objects, artifacts, and other realia there. Writing extends beyond the classroom, too, as kids create small posters for a cause they champion and post these in the hallways.

HOW

LESSON Explore Forms and Purposes

Purpose Kids deepen their understanding of the many reasons why and how we write to communicate, to explore ideas, and to learn.

Engage We bring in a few examples of written forms—postcards, poems, brochures, cartoons, instructions—to build excitement about writing. We create a display of some of our examples, showing the many ways we can share our ideas, and invite kids to bring in their own examples.

Model/Guide We talk about each of the writing forms on display, prompting kids to think about the purpose of each one.

"Here's a _____. Why do you think the author wrote this? Why do you think the illustrator/photographer created or captured this image?

"Here's a _____. Let's read it. What is the message this _____ is trying to communicate to us? That's an important question to ask about whatever we read or view."

As we talk about each form, we remember that drawing and art are aspects of composing, too, so we include and encourage artistic and visual representations.

Practice We invite kids to choose a format and give it a go with information they've been learning or an opinion they want to express.

Share Create and talk about a display of different formats in an ongoing process. Throughout the year we teach these different ways to write in greater detail.

Share a
field guide.

PRACTICE: Share Expertise and Guide Experiences

WHY

A number of essential nonfiction resources provide information about popular topics people want to learn about. Some, like field guides, teach us about rocks and minerals, species of animals (birds, reptiles, and so on), or even medicinal plants. When we visit national parks, nature preserves, museums, monuments, and historical places of interest, we take advantage of others' expertise via guidebooks that enhance our experience.

WHAT

When kids study a wide variety of guides, they learn to write to inform others' experiences. We begin with field guides as the clearest example of this way of gaining knowledge about the world.

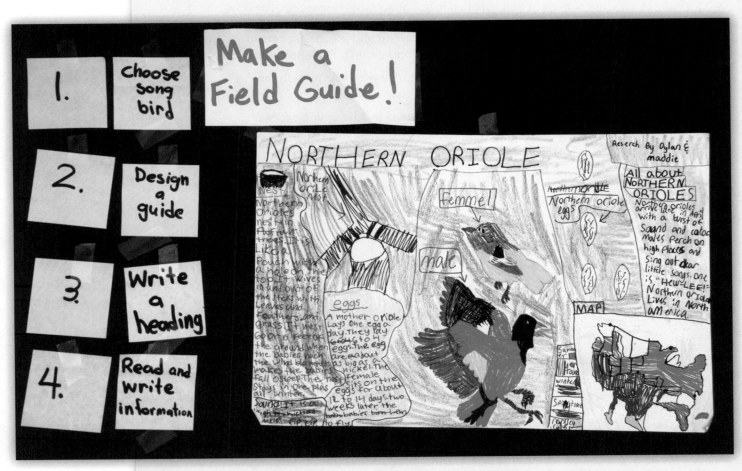

A chart detailing steps for creating a field guide along with the results.

HOW

LESSON Create a Field Guide

Purpose To learn about a variety of field guides and other guidebooks, we use these as mentor texts for writing nonfiction.

Engage Kids pour over a variety of field guides and other guidebooks—and we discuss:

- Why do people use field guides and other kinds of guidebooks?
- Who writes and illustrates these?
- What's in field guides and other guidebooks?

Model/Guide After kids have examined and talked about a number of examples, we zero in on field guides, asking kids what they noticed about them. We observe that the guides include descriptions so we can identify what we are seeing and are written concisely—including important information as well as interesting or unusual details apparent to an observer.

Then we turn to examining the features of a mentor field guide. (We project the image of a page.)

"Here's an example of a field guide page for _____. There are several headings and sections.

"This section gives a specific description of _____. That means people could identify _____ by looking closely at it and comparing what they see to the description in the field guide.

"Here's a section called _____. What do you think we might learn about here?

"This graphic [*map, diagram, photo*] shows us _____. It gives us a really clear view of _____."

Practice "Go ahead and explore one of the field guides. Note what some of the headings are in your particular guide. You'll have to decide which headings you want to use to create a field guide page for your own topic."

Share We list some additional qualities of field guides that we noticed and kids share out their works in progress.

PRACTICE: Distill Information for Easy Access

WHY

Brochures giving health advice, directions for recycling, advertisements for everything under the sun, how-to pamphlets for setting up appliances—this nonfiction genre is ubiquitous, whether printed or online. Having to synthesize information to communicate directions, procedures, and so forth clearly and succinctly gives kids a real-world skill that they can use for many different purposes.

WHAT

We collect many kinds of pamphlets and brochures to use as mentor texts, and we discuss different purposes for writing them. Pamphlets on health and wellness in the doctor's office offer advice on exercise or healthy eating. Safety brochures explain everything from first aid moves to staying safe in extreme weather conditions. Kids need to be very clear about the purpose of the brochure or pamphlet, as they need to include only the most important information, writing and illustrating it in an appealing way so people will pay attention.

This brochure describes a field trip to the National Center for Atmospheric Research (NCAR).

HOW

LESSON Create a Brochure or Pamphlet

Purpose Brochures and pamphlets provide information people need to have at their fingertips.

Engage "Let's think about why we read brochures and pamphlets. Here's one about _____. Notice what's in it. There are photographs of what _____ looks like, where it is located, and what's important about it. The author of this brochure had to decide what was most important to say—and keep it short. Photographs or illustrations make the brochure more appealing and easier to understand."

Model/Guide These are steps for creating a brochure, which we write on a chart.

Planning a Brochure

Think about what you want to teach someone or the directions you want to provide. Ask yourself:

- What is most important to teach?
- What are steps to take to _____?
- What are directions for _____?

Then go ahead and consider:

- What else does the reader need to know to be able to _____?
- If you are giving directions, are they clear and explicit? Could some-one follow them easily?

Practice We tell kids to make sure they answer these planning questions as they go off, sketch out, and finish their own brochures.

Share "We are going to put some of these in the library and the office. Your brochures are about an important and timely topic and people who are waiting in the office or reading in the library may learn important information from them."

PRACTICE: Organize in Sequential Order

WHY

Organizing events in sequential or chronological order happens a lot—whether we are thinking about directions we need to follow, watching a scientific event unfold, or telling a story. Sequencing steps in instructions and procedures is crucial where understanding what to do makes all the difference. Retelling a series of events helps us understand what happened. So whether it's history, science, or everyday life, sequential order makes a difference.

WHAT

Simple narratives—retelling events in history or writing a biography of a person's life—are straightforward ways of summarizing and synthesizing information in the order in which they happened. Time lines of all kinds help kids create a context for historical events, their own lives, or important events they've experienced. The following lesson on time lines helps kids see the big picture as they study history.

A time line created by fourth graders for their study of Colorado history. Paintings of "Colorado 14'ers," mountains over 14,000 feet in altitude, surround the time line.

LESSON Make a Time Line

Purpose To organize information in time order, which provides a big picture of a time period—of someone's life, events in history, etc.

Engage "We're going to think about the most important events for the time period we have been studying. When we create a time line, we use a little text and also images to show how events unfolded. Images and succinct text ensure that our time line gives us a bird's-eye view of what happened over time."

Model/Guide "Thinking about the time period we're studying, we'll put a beginning date on the left and then put an ending date on the far right side, at the end of our time line. Our time line will include important events that happened within this period, between the beginning and ending dates. We want to include the most exciting and important things that happened—we can ask ourselves, 'What do we really want to remember?'

"Let's decide:

o What time increments we'll use—I'll put a mark every five years and add the years in between the beginning and the end of the time line.

o What are the most important events in this period of time? We'll jot these on the time line in the appropriate place. Remember, just a short phrase can describe what happened. So I'll think about the most important information and keep it short.

o We'll double-check the years in which events happened and make sure we accurately place them along the time line.

"We'll add images and visuals to the events we've put on the time line. We can ask ourselves: What image best explains or symbolizes this event?"

Practice When kids go off to practice, we remind them to use images that highlight the information and keep their text short and to the point.

Share Kids come together to share and respond to each other's time lines in progress.

PRACTICE: Write to Persuade

WHY

The last step in the inquiry framework is Take Public—and often Take Public also means Take Action. Often persuasive writing, using facts from research, is the key to making a difference. Kids marshal the information they have learned throughout the inquiry to support their position and make their voices heard.

WHAT

Editorials, essays, picket signs, advertisements, letters, and so on all have the potential for changing hearts and minds. Many are accessible to kids. As we guide kids to think strategically about persuasion, we ask them to

- Think about something that concerns them, an important issue, a problem, or a lingering question.

- Think about reasons why they are concerned. What information do they already know about the issue or problem? Accurate information is evidence that they can use to support their opinion.

- Express an opinion, backed by information and evidence, to persuade someone to understand our concern or opinion.

- In the following lesson, a persuasive letter provides a way into the basics of persuasion—taking a position, giving reasons to support it, and backing up reasons with facts or evidence.

After researching specific species of sea turtles, kids voice their concerns by creating and sharing persuasive posters.

HOW

LESSON Write a Persuasive Letter

Purpose To write a persuasive letter that takes a position and supports it with compelling reasons and researched information (see p. 201 for an example).

Engage The class has just completed an inquiry. Current events related to what kids have been studying—the environment, a historical monument, a newly registered endangered species, an incident of civil unrest—often appear in thought-provoking articles. After reading an article on a topic about which kids have a lot of information, they express strong opinions.

Model/Guide Several kids are eager to respond with their opinions about the article so we discuss writing persuasive letters and think about who we should write to: The author of the article? The subject of the article? Someone mentioned in the article? Once we've decided on the audience, we co-construct a chart of steps for writing a persuasive letter.

Steps for Writing a Persuasive Letter

- State your opinion or position on an issue.
- Explain the reasons for your concern, including evidence and information that supports your position or opinion.
- Think about polite and respectful language that will help persuade someone to agree with or support your position/opinion.

Practice "Now it's your turn. You may not all have the same opinion or position on this issue. As you write a draft of your own letter, be sure to look back at our chart about the steps we can follow in composing it. Remember to think about what will be most effective in getting your ideas across and encouraging the recipient of the letter to understand your position."

Share In subsequent lessons, we teach the format of a letter and research the appropriate recipients before kids prepare their final drafts. Then we mail them, the ultimate share.

> *"Illustration is composition. What if we can support children as they make meaning both visually and verbally and know that in doing so, neither ability or competency is diminished?"*
> —Katie Wood Ray

Incorporate Design Elements

There are myriad ways to compose nonfiction using words, images, and other features. Kids make decisions about text and graphics as they create the pages of a picture book as well as every other kind of nonfiction. We model making decisions about the ways in which illustrations highlight and elaborate on presented facts. We demonstrate how a variety of design features encourage the reader to interact with the text. All of these become options as kids expand their nonfiction repertoire.

We often introduce and kids use these elements of design in both writer's and researcher's workshops:

Practice	Why is this foundational to writer's workshop?	How is it applied in researcher's workshop?
Capture Information in Words and Pictures *Lesson:* Make a Teaching Book	Composing in words and pictures gives kids opportunities to write what they want to write and draw. Self-published picture books are an ideal entry point—so kids learn to "build ideas across the pages of books" (Ray 2008).	Researchers become specialists in their own topics. They blend writing and drawing to create their own original take on something they know a lot about.
Make Ideas Pop *Lesson:* Create a 3-D Mural	"Working big" engages kids. Inventive ways kids can express their ideas include large illustrations with labels and captions, life-size models, interactive displays.	Accuracy matters when presenting research. Kids turn the new information they are learning into scenes, murals, Lego creations, and other projects that teach the viewer and reader.
Represent Complex Ideas with Graphics *Lesson:* Create an Infographic	Thinking is sometimes more easily expressed through pictures rather than words. Kids learn that images, graphics, and text all work together to get the writer's ideas across.	Informational text is chock-full of images and photos, graphics, videos, and the like. Learning from these models, kids create ways in which visuals and text can work together to inform.
Blend Writing, Art, and Design *Lesson:* Enliven Information with Design Techniques	Design makes a difference. Showing kids how to plan out how they incorporate illustrations and graphics (images, diagrams, maps, close-ups, etc.) requires them to pay close attention to the best way to communicate their message.	When researchers envision ways to share content, having a toolbox of design features at their fingertips can make a big difference in engaging the audience and informing others. Options give kids the best shot at writing and creating with invention and imagination.

PRACTICE: Capture Information in Words and Pictures

WHY

In many genres, images—photos, illustrations, and sketches—work with text to create an informative whole. Some young writers think first in pictures, then in words—or vice versa. As kids match their pictures and words, they create a coherent piece. Illustrations often lead the way as kids "build ideas across the pages of books" (Ray 2009, 14), expressing themselves as developing writers and artists.

WHAT

Picture books, cartoons, comics, posters, and photo essays are just a few of the genres that kids can write to hone their picture–text strategy. After an inquiry, picture books can be a good way to summarize what information most intrigued kids or what they most recall. In this lesson, kids create teaching books, deciding what to include by thinking about what they know or are specialists in and creating a self-published book.

Kids share teaching books about birds.

HOW

LESSON Make a Teaching Book

Purpose Kids build their independence as writers as they teach others about information or topics they are eager to share. Teaching books are picture books on topics that kids are passionate about and know a lot about (Harvey and Goudvis 2017).

Engage "Let's take a look at some of these picture books authored by kids. Kids wrote about what they were interested in and knew a lot about. For example, here is a picture about snakes. You can see the author wrote about and illustrated several different kinds of snakes and wrote a caption about each one. You all are specialists, too. What do you know about?"

Model/Guide We guide kids to write a teaching book:

"For example, Lydia is a _____ specialist. She wrote a teaching/picture book about them. The most important thing about a teaching book is that

- You care about the topic.
- You are a specialist and know a lot about the topic.
- You have information that you are eager to share, and you write and draw what you know.

"Here are the steps we can use to write a picture book. I'll jot these on a chart that you can refer to as you create a picture book":

- Think of important information you want to teach someone through writing and drawing.
- Staple some pages together.
- Begin drawing and writing on the first page—you can begin with either writing or drawing.
- Think about the next thing you want to write about. Be sure your words and illustrations match.
- When you are finished, ask yourself: Is there anything else that's important to include in a book about _____?
- Create a cover and add the title of your book.

"Turn and talk with someone near you and share your topic. Tell them about what you will write about in your book."

Practice Kids go off with a set of pages to create their own teaching books.

Share Kids come back and share their books. As kids read their books to one or two peers, they glean ideas from each other.

Take It Further There are many forms of picture books. We bring in a number of different kinds of mentor texts that illustrate different styles of picture books.

PRACTICE: Make Ideas Pop

WHY

Posters, large-scale murals, life-size model displays, and the like give kids plenty of space to work and room to embellish. They are a fun way for them to present what they know. Kids love working big, and once they understand how they can share their new learning in this way, they often choose this means of expressing themselves.

WHAT

Big presentation forms are usually created as ways of distilling and communicating after kids have studied a topic for a while. In preparation, kids put together Post-its that record new learning, illustrate salient information, and write what they learned. These may become part of a poster or mural or display or be transcribed in new ways. The work can be fairly simple or complex and becomes more sophisticated and informative over time, encompassing a variety of design techniques to make the final product engaging and interactive.

A three-dimensional rain forest mural with a flowing stream, trees, and plants creates an environment for kids to add the animals that live in different rain forest habitats, for example, the canopy and the forest floor. This brings the habitat to life.

HOW

LESSON Create a 3–D Mural

Purpose Create spaces to record thinking and take it public with art and text.

Engage We ask what kids know about murals and collaborate to explain what a mural is: a big wall display that captures a scene, an event, or an experience.

Model/Guide "We're creating a scene about _____. We've read books and watched videos, and now we'll put all this information into our mural. What do we need to make sure we include?"

- Accurate drawings and illustrations: Make these big enough for your viewer to see and learn from. You can use paper, cardboard, cloth, or other materials to make 3-D features.
- Captions and labels for your drawings: Make sure these accurately describe what you have illustrated.
- The scene your mural creates: For example, rather than just drawing leaves, you can make them out of paper so they look real and are three-dimensional.
- Features and design techniques: Use a variety of these (for example, pop-ups or sliders to show movement; see the lesson 'Enliven Information with Design Techniques') to make your illustrations and text more interesting.

Practice We "build" the mural together over several days. Kids create their contributions—labeling, writing captions, and making features to represent the information.

Share We share the 3-D mural. Children come from other classrooms to listen and view as the creators share their expertise.

PRACTICE: Represent Complex Ideas with Graphics

WHY

We teach kids to distill information into graphic forms that are clear and easy to understand. Websites filled with images and videos, viral photo memes, infographics—all are designed to present information graphically in an attractive and easy-to-grasp format. Challenging kids to present key concepts is a great way to promote deep processing of information.

WHAT

The sample lesson on the next page teaches kids to create infographics, a twenty-first-century skill if ever there was one. The questions that guide the writer's decisions on how to create an infographic work for any graphic presentation of information:

- What's the purpose of this infographic/commercial/ad? To inform? Persuade? What are the big ideas or the message?

- What information and ideas make sense to write as text? As images?

- What images and illustrations will show your information or message?

- How will the text and visual images work together?

HOW

LESSON Create an Infographic

Purpose To distill, illustrate, and share information in a graphic form.

Engage "To get ready to create an infographic ourselves, let's review the chart we made about infographics. We'll keep these things in mind as we create our own."

Feature	Quality
Text	
• Title	Concise and catchy
• Captions, labels	Short; explain the visual images
Images	
• Photos, diagrams, illustrations	Capture the main subject of the infographic
• Close-ups	Show important details
• Cross sections	Show what's inside something
Devices	
• Arrows	Show direction or movement
• Bold print	Signals importance
• Vivid colors	Eye-catching; match the message

Model/Guide "Let's sketch out a plan for an infographic. For example, let's think about how we could create an infographic to explain _____." (*We sketch a rough plan as we think through these features.*)

"First, I'll think about the purpose and the information I want to share and jot my **title** right here at the top. My images need to show the topic, so I'll think about what **illustrations** and **images** I'll need to find or draw.

"If I'm showing a something that has a lot of action, I'll think about **devices** I can use. Maybe arrows or maybe a flap that shows before on the front of the flap and after inside the flap. Or maybe I'll include several frames that show a sequence.

"Now I'll think about the colors I'll use. What colors go best with my topic?

"And finally I'll add a section about interesting facts, just a list."

Practice We remind kids to think about the purpose of their infographic first: to inform or to persuade, or perhaps another goal. They each create a rough, visual sketch or draft of their infographic.

Share After we each share, we give one another feedback on our draft or sketch. Kids incorporate these suggestions as they continue to create their infographic.

PRACTICE: Blend Writing, Art, and Design

WHY

We teach kids a variety of artistic and design techniques for creating information-filled, accurate, engaging projects of all kinds. They apply these techniques to any product: self-published books, posters, mind maps, and so forth. Once kids understand different ways of expressing information artistically and creating it with paper, cardboard, and other materials, they can design almost anything they can envision.

WHAT

A mix of written and artistic devices is as much fun for the creator to imagine and make as it is for the reader to learn from. Interactive features—for example, flaps that open, pop-ups, sliders—engage readers and convey information.

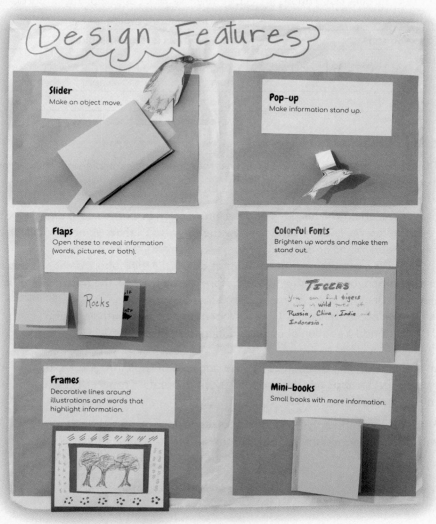

Examples illustrate a variety of design techniques.

HOW

LESSON Enliven Information with Design Techniques

Purpose Kids combine embedded mini-books, flaps, sliders, and other interactive features with words to convey information, using their imaginations to show and demonstrate their learning.

Engage "It is really interesting to see the design techniques you all are using as you write and illustrate your research topics. With these devices, you are adding accurate details that make your poster or book much more engaging and informative to read!"

Model/Guide "Let's investigate some new possibilities. For example, I can use a flap to show the outside and inside of _____. On the outside of the flap, I'll draw what lives outside. When we lift the flap, we'll see what's living inside, so I'll draw the inside picture under the flap. I could add labels and captions, too. Flaps can also demonstrate what happens first and then next. I'll need to put clear details on the front of the flap, and then what happens next on the inside of the flap.

"Here's another design technique; we call this a *slider*. It shows action—so think about what on your poster could be moving around and you could try this technique. To make a slider, let's first draw whatever will be moving. If we cut a slit in the poster, we can put the slider part behind and see just the part we want the reader to see. It's really a demonstration—right on your poster!"

Practice Kids think for a minute about what design technique they would like to try. We remind them to think about the information they want to share and the technique that best matches it.

Share As kids share out their design techniques, they pick up ideas about what to try from one another.

> *"It is not enough to simply teach children to read; we have to give them something worth reading. Something that will stretch their imaginations—something that will help them make sense of their own lives and encourage them to reach out toward people whose lives are quite different from their own."*
>
> —Katherine Patterson,
> *A Sense of Wonder*

When we blend reading and writing with inquiry, here's what can happen . . .

Twenty-six expectant second graders gather on the rug, eager for read-aloud time. We begin, "Sometimes when we read a book, it reflects our own experiences so that we make connections to our own lives. Other times, books carry us away to new adventures. Let's see what happens as we read this book, which is one of my favorites. It's called *Maybe Something Beautiful*, and at first I wondered what that title means. The book begins in the middle of a city, which looks dark and drab, with gray buildings. It certainly doesn't seem very beautiful right now.

"Listen carefully as I stop and share my inner conversation with you. I'll jot down my thoughts and questions about it. Remember to listen to your inner voice as I read, and then you can talk about, sketch, and draw your own inner conversation, and share it with all of us. After we finish reading, you'll have a chance to draw and write your reflections and responses to the story."

> In the heart of a gray city, there lived a girl who loved to doodle, draw, color and paint. Every time she saw a blank piece of paper, Mira thought to herself, "Hmm, maybe . . ." And because of this her room was filled with color and her heart was filled with joy.

"I'm noticing the illustrations on this page. From the gray and black drawings of the buildings, I infer that the city is a dreary place. It reminds me of when I lived in the city, where in the winter everything, even the trees, looked dull and drab. But Mira, the young girl in the story, has some different ideas. Hmm . . . what are you thinking? Turn and talk."

Kids burst with ideas: "When Mira draws, the colors make her happy."
"She's giving out her paintings! I think she wants to make friends."
"Mira's spreading joy!"

As the story unfolds, Mira meets a fellow artist, who helps her inspire the whole neighborhood to take action. The kids are amazed when we read the last part of the book, with photographs of the true story on which the book is based: people making murals, painting buildings wild colors, livening up their neighborhood, and building a vibrant community along the way.

Kids are inspired—and as they read and respond to this story, Gerardo exclaims: "I have an idea! Maybe we could do what Mira did. We could paint pictures and give them to people." So we do, and give them to delighted staff around the school. We wonder if there are other ways to make our world more beautiful, so we search for other ideas, reading **The Curious Garden**, where kids learn about Liam, a child in New York City, who nurtures and grows plants to fill his neighborhood with natural beauty. We meet Miss Rumphius, who spread flowers everywhere that "made the world more beautiful."

"Why couldn't we do that at our school?" someone chimes in. Indeed, why couldn't we do that? So we do.

Powerful picture books, as Rudine Sims Bishop says, become both mirrors and windows for readers. Kids need to see themselves reflected in the books they read. But even more important, books become windows and pathways for kids to experience a diverse and complex world, just as Katherine Patterson suggests.

We read <u>Maybe Something Beautiful.</u>

Brown Color

This story makes me think......

I Think That She
is goweTo Mak
her Tawn MoRe
Beeoutefol

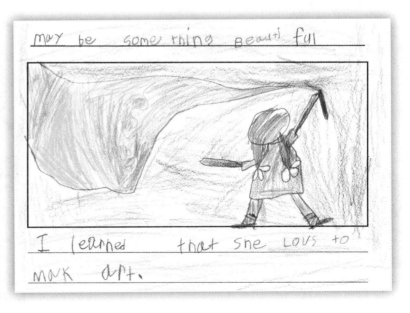

may be some thing Beautiful

I learned that she Lovs to
Mak art.

Kids care for and nurture plants in the school greenhouse.

Kids create a small garden outside the classroom and care for it.

Inquiry Across the Grades

· ·

"Always be on the lookout for the presence of wonder."

—E. B. White

In this chapter, we take you on a journey through grades one to four. These inquiries follow the frameworks and teach the same research process we've described.

Just like the scrapbook or photo collection (real or virtual) created after a memorable vacation, inquiry in the researcher's workshop is as much about the journey as the destination. You've read (and we hope followed) the detailed road map we've provided in the two previous chapters, "Researcher's Workshop" and "Reading and Writing in Support of Inquiry." You've watched video snippets of kids in classrooms that buzz and hum with student voice, energy, and wonder. Whether short and sweet like the first-grade cultural inquiry or more complex like the fourth-grade inquiry on understanding different perspectives in history, these examples paint a picture and provide a spark for your own ways of implementing researcher's workshop across the grades in your school.

Cultural Inquiry in the First Grade

"Wow, those sandals are hard to walk in. I almost fell over."

"I love the red ones. Look, they are called tabi."

"I love this kimono! But do they wear these to school?"

"How would they play in a kimono?"

"Is that sushi in the picture?"

"What is sushi anyway?"

"It's fish!"

"Look at that photo—look at all the fish!"

"That's a lot of fish."

Young children study other cultures to build awareness of and knowledge about people and traditions from around the world. Essential questions and enduring understandings are focused on exploring many aspects of a culture. Kids' authentic questions become the focus for their research.

Enduring Understandings

In this increasingly interconnected world, kids learn that people around the world have different cultural practices, languages, traditions, and experiences. Kids are intrigued to find out about similarities and differences with respect to food, clothing, language, literature, and other aspects of life. The EUs and EQs are about Japan but are transferable to all cultures.

Essential Questions

- What is life like in this culture?
- What can we find out about schools, family life, food, sports, clothing, transportation, stories and poetry, traditions, and celebrations?
- What are the differences and similarities between life here in the U.S. and in this culture?

Kids are curious about and interact with all sorts of artifacts. The more kids learn, the more they wonder.

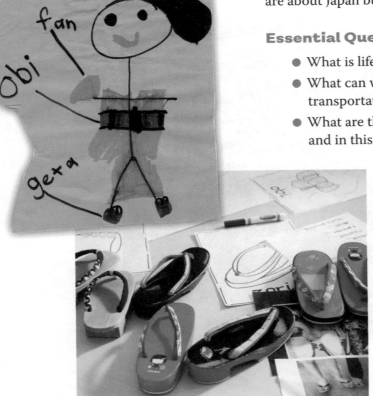

IMMERSE

Learn new information and wonder about photos, videos, and artifacts. Kids explore Japanese objects, try on clothing, and experiment with writing and art supplies. They view videos and listen to read-alouds that introduce different aspects of Japanese culture. Their conversations spark authentic questions for research.

Use literature as an entry point into Japanese culture, traditions, and ideas. Listening to read-alouds of stories and folktales transport kids to other times and places. This adds to their understanding of life in Japan as well as its rich traditions.

Experiences prompt questions in ways reading may not. Kids view photographs about sports in Japan, wearing headbands (*hachimaki*). These headbands stand for perseverance and hard work and are often worn for sporting events or by anyone taking pride in their work.

Essential questions frame the Japan inquiry:

- What is life like in Japan?
- What can we find out about Japanese schools, family life, food, sports, clothing, transportation, stories and poetry, traditions and celebrations?
- What are the differences and similarities between life here in the U.S. and Japan?

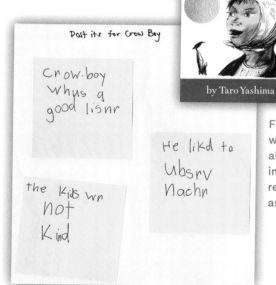

Post its for Crow Boy

Crow.boy
whas a
good lisnr

He likd to
ubsrv
nachr

the kids wr
not
kind

First graders engage with folktales and also discuss and infer the messages in realistic fiction, such as *Crow Boy*.

Crow Boy
by Taro Yashima

INVESTIGATE

Kids research answers to their questions. Read-alouds, videos, photos, realia, and group discussions give kids the grist for answering—or figuring out the answers to—their questions. A wide range of books with many photographs and images provide information kids are eager to learn about.

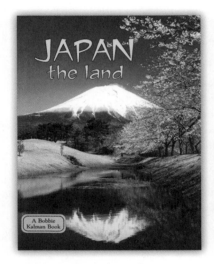

Kids read a variety of texts and view videos about daily life in Japan to discover answers to their questions.

Kids revisit artifacts with a fourth grader who has lived in Japan and is fluent in Japanese. She models how to answer questions about clothing, explaining in English and writing about clothing in Japanese.

COALESCE

Visualize: Read and write free-form poems evoked by images. Short poems, mainly haiku, accompany paintings and illustrations often about nature. Kids listen to poems and visualize the images that come to mind. Hearing poems read aloud about cherry blossoms in the spring or Mt. Fuji looming in the distance inspires kids to create their own sketches of what they imagine, based on the words of the poem. Then they create their own poems.

First graders view paintings and photos and write their own short poems describing the images.

TAKE PUBLIC

Share poetry. First graders learn about the tradition of placing poems in trees for celebration. They tie small versions of poems they have written into the trees outside the library to share with families at the end of the school day.

After reading poetry and writing their own poems, kids decide to hang their poems in trees in the spirit of the Japanese tradition.

Celebrate. Going public doesn't always have to be a poster or project. Kids enjoy a Japanese extravaganza, complete with a sushi-making and -tasting session, lessons in writing their names in Kanji, and creating origami.

Kids interview a sushi chef and restaurant owner with their questions about sushi.

Biography in Second Grade

In language arts, author and genre studies lend themselves to a researcher's workshop approach. Binge reading multiple books or a series by a favorite author is a surefire way to hook kids into a reading habit. A genre study can do the same. Once kids become familiar with a genre—picture book, biography, sci-fi, mystery, and so on—they naturally gravitate toward books in a genre that captures their interest.

This inquiry on biography, organized about picture-book biographies of environmentalists, serves two goals simultaneously. It extends kids' understanding of their ongoing science inquiry and it introduces them to biographies.

Enduring Understandings

A biography tells the story of a person's life and experiences.
From a biography we learn about a person's important contributions to the world and why we remember them.

Essential Questions

- Why do we remember this person?
- How did he or she make a difference in the world?
- What did she or he do to make the world a better place?

Kids choose a good-fit biography and read with the essential questions in mind.

IMMERSE

Respond during an interactive read-aloud. We launch the inquiry with an interactive read-aloud. "When we read about famous people, we often think about why we remember them. These books, all biographies, are about people who made contributions to the world. That means they worked to make the world a better place for all of us. People can make a difference in many ways: They take action to protect the environment, for example, or they fight for social justice so that people are treated fairly and equally. Other people—such as artists, musicians, or poets—contribute their talents and creativity to make the world a more beautiful, welcoming place filled with art, poetry, and song."

Listening to the biography *Wangari's Trees of Peace*, kids learn that Wangari Maathai inspired Kenyans to take better care of their environment by starting a tree-planting movement that revitalized the African countryside and eventually won Maathai the Nobel Peace Prize. During reading, these essential questions guide our thinking:

Essential questions about Wangari

- Why do we remember Wangari?
- How did Wangari make a difference?
- What did she do to make the world a better place?

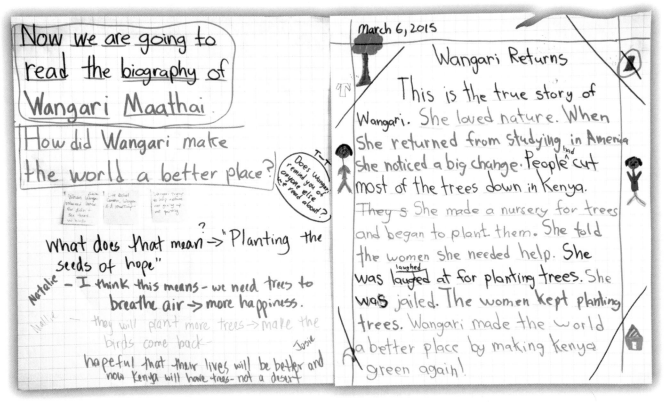

Together, the class creates a summary of Wangari's accomplishments on a large chart, responding to the essential questions.

INVESTIGATE

Read independently. After reading, responding to, and summarizing Wangari's contributions, kids choose their own biography. With multiple copies and a wide variety of options, kids read about someone who piques their interest. Kids who choose the same biography gravitate together, creating informal book clubs. They discuss the essential questions as they read.

Talk with our pens. The life story of another environmental activist, John Muir, catches our attention. We read a picture-book biography aloud, thinking about our essential questions and how Muir's story is connected to others we have read.

Students typically have face-to-face conversations about the books they are reading; another approach is to hold a conversation in writing. In a written conversation, kids read what their peers have written and respond with their own comments or questions. Writing a comment encourages them to "listen" carefully and take a little more time to thoughtfully respond to one another's comments (Volpat 2009).

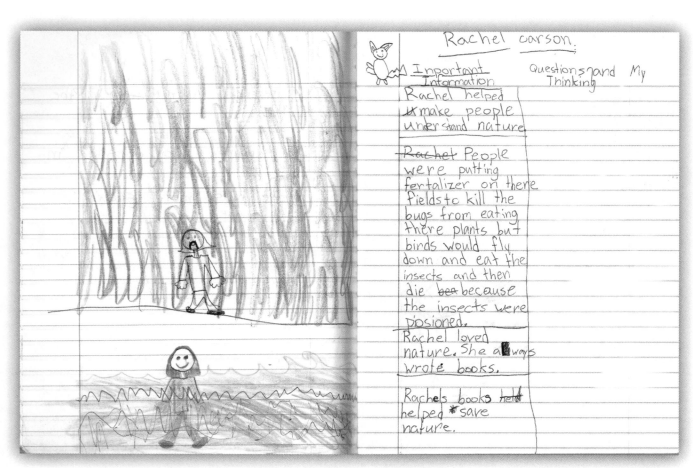

Journal entry about Rachel Carson and what she did to make a difference

Coached ahead of time, a small group of students models what to do. Their peers observe them as they

- write comments about the text
- respond directly to someone else's idea, question, or connection
- add their own learning, wondering, or other
- pass the page to the next person.

Then everyone has a go in small groups.

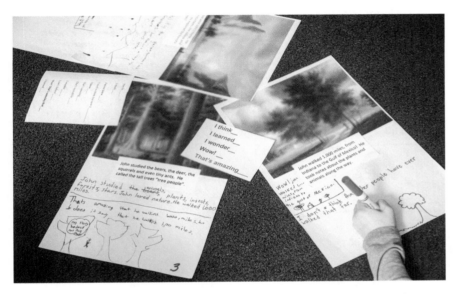

Kids read the previous entries and add their own comments and sketches. They use different-colored pens to make it clear where one response ends and the next begins. They include questions that others respond to as part of the written conversation.

Written Conversations
We have lots of conversations!
Now we're going to talk with our pens!

You'll write:
- what you notice
- what you learned
- a question
- ask the next person "What do you think?"

View
1
read
2
write
3
pass
4

An anchor chart guides kids through the procedure for having a written conversation.

View, read, write, and pass again.

COALESCE/TAKE PUBLIC

Summarize ideas across texts. Returning to the essential questions about why we remember people and how they have made a difference, we look back at our charts and think about different environmentalists. Kids summarize their learning about people who were environmental activists.

Kids make connections between Wangari Maathai's efforts to plant trees in Kenya and Rachel Carson's efforts to save the environment.

This child shared scientist Maria Merian's discovery of the butterfly life cycle in the 1600s.

How did John James Audubon test his ideas? What observations did he make? What 🔲 experiments did he do?

John James studied Birds all day in a cave he tied string to the chics feet his main Question was do birds come back to the same place?

JOHN MUIR

• John John Muir lived in Scotland. he came to the U.S. he walked 1,000 miles writing notes as he went. then, after a while, he came to. yosemite. he loved writing in his notebook. Soon, he relized people were cutting down forests. So he wrote a book to stop it.

John John started the Sierra club to save and study nature. he became a father to 2 girls.

Kids summarize and share thinking about biographies and continue their research with people they want to learn about.

Thinking Like Scientists Inquiry in Second Grade

Here's the thing: If kids don't dwell in content long enough, questions may never surface and big ideas can remain elusive or locked away. By learning about animals and issues surrounding their survival, kids come to better understand and care about the environment. This spills over into studying scientists and their passion for the world and what they do. Because kids care, there is a sense of urgency to find out what's happening and why.

The researcher's workshop takes a new twist: investigating how scientists think, study, and explore the world. Kids learn what scientists do, including the tools they use, experiments they conduct, and how they record their findings and take their knowledge public. Essential questions and enduring understandings focus on kids learning about the passion and curiosity that fuel scientific discoveries as well as the scientific process that leads to new understandings about the world.

Neil DeGrasse Tyson reminds us that the scientific method follows these simple rules:

1. Test ideas by experiment and observation.
2. Build on those ideas that pass the test; reject the ones that fail.
3. Follow the evidence wherever it leads.
4. Question everything.

As kids learn about and from a particular scientist, they find out how this person acted on his or her curiosity, explored mysteries and questions, persisted in the face of challenges, and made significant contributions. Kids study the ways in which the scientists observed, gathered evidence, and posed questions about the natural world. Through this inquiry, students expand their research repertoire.

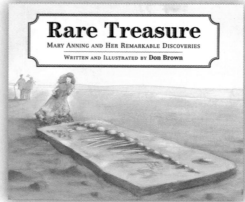
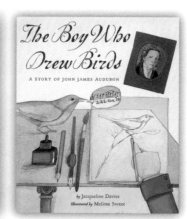

HOW SCIENTISTS THINK AND LEARN

SCIENTISTS		Discovery	Observation	Experiments	Action	Big Idea
	William Bentley	Willie discovered that the crystal structures of snowflakes vary with the temperature (below freezing).	Willie looked at close-ups of snowflakes; difficult to capture them for study, so he took photographs with a special camera to have a permanent record.	Willie tried different methods to take pictures of snowflakes. He learned that their structures varied with temperature and described how.	sketching photographing publishing presenting Willie published the still definitive work on how snowflake structures vary in relation to temperature.	The form and structure of snowflakes change according to temperature.
	Mary Anning	Mary sought out fossils; she became an early collector who studied them scientifically.	Mary found and observed fossil remains in their natural states; realized the importance of studying the context in which fossils are found to learn about them.		sketching presenting studying collecting Mary displayed fossils and gave talks about her finds and methods. She is considered to be the one of the first woman paleontologists.	Fossils tell Earth's history.
	John James Audubon	John James discovered migratory patterns of birds; discovered and experimented with observations that confirmed his theories about bird behavior.	John James listened and noticed birds in their habitat.	John James tied thread to banded birds to see if they returned. They did and this established evidence of his theories of migration.	sketching painting listening studying publishing John James' published sketches, paintings, and writing continue to serve as models for naturalists to share knowledge in many fields of study.	Birds migrate in winter and follow predictable routes.

This inquiry focuses on the work of three scientists, each anchored in a picture book about the scientist's life. The chart on the previous page distills the key ideas about how the scientists pursued their passions. The texts build on DeGrasse Tyson's ideas about scientists and the scientific method. As kids observe, study, and record their learning, they take a crack at becoming scientists themselves (Heisey and Kucan 2011).

Essential questions and enduring understandings are transferable: We pose similar questions and understandings for each scientist.

Enduring Understandings

- Scientists wonder about and observe the natural world.
- They conduct experiments, study, record, and publish information.
- We can do what scientists do and learn about their fields of study.
- We use scientific methods to learn about the process of scientific discovery.

Essential Questions

- What is a scientist?
- How do scientists think, observe, record, and take public what they learn?
- What were the scientist's passions and interests?
- What were his or her contributions to the world?
- What challenges did he or she face?

After interactive read-alouds and learning about different scientists, this second grader writes and draws in response to questions about John James Audubon's scientific discoveries.

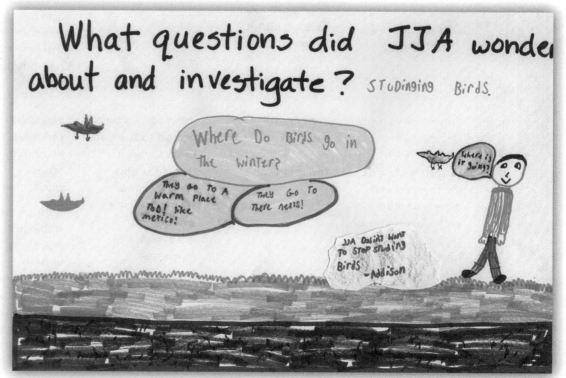

William "Snowflake" Bentley

As an example, we describe one of the three inquiries in this series: a study of weather, with William "Snowflake" Bentley as the model scientist.

> Essential Questions About "Snowflake" Bentley
> • What did he do and think about as a scientist?
> • What was he interested in and passionate about?
> • What contributions did he make to the world?
> • What challenges did he face?

IMMERSE

Explore resources and materials. Kids view resources and explore artifacts to build their intrigue about the topic of weather. Models of giant hailstones, engaging photographs, books, and online sources (especially video) about extreme weather events inspire kids' questions and build their background knowledge about weather events.

Read *Snowflake Bentley*. For an interactive read-aloud of *Snowflake Bentley*, kids sit up close with Post-Its and clipboards, so they can write their thoughts and questions about the story as they listen to it. They learn about Snowflake Bentley's life, how he studied and investigated his passion for all things snow, and his contributions as a scientist. Kids discover what Snowflake Bentley did to observe the natural world, noting that he used his eyes and mind to carefully observe what was going on around him. They discuss and respond to essential questions that guide the read-aloud (see above). They notice the qualities that made Willie a thoughtful and successful researcher, determined to follow his passion.

Kids marvel over a giant hailstone, asking questions and wondering how it could have grown so large.

INVESTIGATE

Study the science of snow. Studying photographs and the structure of snow crystals launches kids into the study of snow and snowflakes, just like Snowflake Bentley. When it snows, kids go outside with black construction paper and capture snowflakes, observing the crystal structures they are studying. They have learned that "the snowflake's size and shape change if it's warmer or colder."

To emulate Snowflake Bentley, kids access the National Oceanic and Atmospheric Administration's (NOAA) website section about how to be citizen scientists and submit weather observations on NOAA's free app, mPING. Anyone can submit a weather observation anonymously, and the data immediately go into a database at NOAA and the National Severe Storms Laboratory. It is then shown live on the app.

We investigate the science of snow, just like Willie did, examining the different kinds of ice crystals that form snowflakes using Willie's snowflake research and other materials.

NOAA website illustrating "citizen scientist" data

Conduct experiments. Kids design an experiment to measure how snow melts depending on its location. They venture outside and measure snow depths in sunny locations and compare them to areas that get no sun, creating a graph to record the depths of snow in sun versus shade.

Investigate weather and how it affects people. Considering another essential question (*How does weather affect people?*), kids investigate specific kinds of weather events—the more extreme, the better. Dramatic weather is sure to capture their interest! Kids explore tornadoes, hurricanes, blizzards, and other forms of extreme weather.

VIDEO CLIP

Research an essential question.

Each snow scientist measures the snow in centimeters and then we average the data.

Back in the classroom we discuss our evidence, writing up snow measurements for various places in the courtyard. Where did the snow melt the most? Why? Kids write up the results on a big chart.

"Poster texts" provide comprehensible and accessible information and images about specific weather events.

COALESCE/TAKE PUBLIC

At this point in the year, kids have many options for organizing and sharing their new knowledge. These options have been collected on a researcher's workshop menu of ways to take learning public:

- self-published picture books
- posters
- mind maps
- poems
- museum exhibits
- digital books
- brochures and pamphlets.

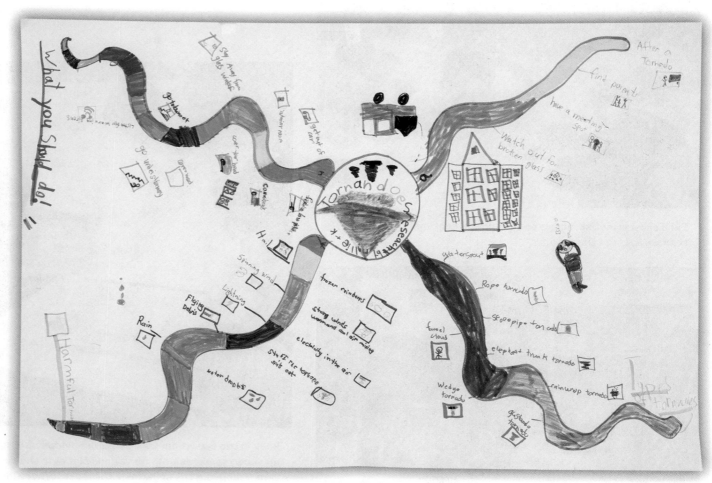

This mind map includes different types of tornadoes, such as rope and elephant trunk tornadoes, and what to do to stay safe.

The NOAA tornado brochure is a mentor text for creating our own brochures.

Kids realize how dangerous tornadoes are and create brochures that advise people what to do to stay safe.

Kids share brochures about tornado safety.

Brad teaches art strategies like shading with pastels make learning big and visible to engage readers.

When brochures are completed, they are displayed in the school office to inform others about ways to stay safe during a tornado.

National Parks Inquiry in Third Grade

When third graders studying our national parks heard the news, they spoke out. Looking at a map of the downsized Bears Ears National Monument in southeastern Utah, they exclaimed: "What?!! Bears Ears used to be this big and now it's like *this*?"

"How can they just take away a million acres of it? They should have left it like it was."

"I thought this was Native American land! Did anyone ask them?"

Kids learned about the history of Bears Ears National Monument, 1.35 million acres in southeastern Utah designated through the efforts of five native tribes in concert with the Obama administration in December 2016. They read several differing perspectives on the presidential decision, one year later in December 2017, to shrink the Bears Ears National Monument by 85 percent. Kids weren't shy about weighing in with their opinions.

Investigating some of the current controversies surrounding the national parks and monuments engages kids in real-world issues. With teacher guidance, kids came up with questions about parks they chose to investigate. By third grade, kids were very familiar with the research process: exploring sources, investigating questions, and synthesizing their new learning. Appropriately, the emphasis in this inquiry is on kids' own projects and taking these public.

This national parks inquiry addresses district standards as well as the third-grade social studies curriculum focusing on U.S. regions. Studying parks and monuments in various geographical regions, kids also learned about the environmental stewardship that ensures the parks' continued existence.

The following enduring understandings and essential questions guide the study.

Enduring Understandings

- Caring for our national parks preserves unique geographical areas, important archaeological and historical artifacts and areas, and unspoiled places. Parks are a valuable and irreplaceable resource.
- Parks are representative of important regional geographic and geologic features, habitats, natural wonders, and so on.
- There are differing perspectives on the purposes of our national park system. Tourism, recreation, and economic development for a region may compete with preserving wild and natural places.

Essential Questions

- How is this national park an important example of the environment (for example, geographic and geological features) of this region?
- What are the unique natural features of this park? What recreational and historical aspects are worth a visit and what kinds of experiences might one have there?
- What different perspectives, controversies, and actions are important to consider when thinking about the future of our national parks?
- What actions might we take to preserve these "national treasures"?

Kids explore books, videos, and websites to build their knowledge about national parks.

Kids pore over images and take virtual tours of several national parks to pique their questions and build background about their history and natural features.

Create "thick" and "thin" questions for research.

IMMERSE/INVESTIGATE

Locate and explore specific parks. To explore the topic and build background knowledge about national parks, kids watch sections of Ken Burns' video series *The National Parks: America's Best Idea.* They begin to appreciate the beauty and variety of these scenic places, which they locate on a U.S. map.

Explore sources and begin to develop questions for research. As a model for their own reading and research, kids read the *National Geographic Ladders National Parks* book about the Grand Canyon and consider these questions, specific versions of the essential questions on the previous page.

- What geological features of the Grand Canyon are typical of the southwest region of the United States?
- What are some of the unique and interesting natural features within the park? What places would I like to visit?
- What recreational opportunities (hiking, rock climbing, boating, fishing) are there in Grand Canyon National Park?
- Are there any current issues or controversies surrounding the Grand Canyon National Park?
- What does the future hold for this park?

Librarian Melissa Oviatt collaborates with teacher Erin Livingston to read and discuss questions for research.

Annotate text and images. Kids take notes on texts, images, videos, and websites. Modeling how to read and annotate print and digital texts, teachers reiterate strategies such as paraphrasing, asking questions, making inferences, and connecting to background knowledge.

Third graders choose from several note-taking options. They jot down new learning and questions.

COALESCE/TAKE ACTION

Create projects. After investigating a park or monument of their choosing, kids decide how to share their knowledge with a larger audience. Kids seek out photos, maps, and website information for slide show presentations. One pair creates a video of the Statue of Liberty and in the process also learn about the events of September 11, 2001. Two kids report on the Lincoln Memorial.

An interactive map created by third-grade teacher Steve Ollanik allows interested readers to access each online project. When kids have plenty of choice and latitude for sharing their knowledge and speaking out in their own ways, they become researchers in the fullest sense.

An introduction to a slide show about the Everglades National Park

An interactive map shows the location of the national parks and monuments that kids investigated.

Kid-created video about the Statue of Liberty

Express opinions and speak out. After delving into their own parks or monuments, kids have a stake in their preservation. They research some of the issues that arise as Congress and other government agencies consider how to support (or not) our national parks. Some kids choose to craft opinion pieces and/or letters about issues connected to their particular park. They speak out for a cause they know about and have come to care about. What better way to encourage future citizens who will speak out and stand up?

"Keep close to Nature's heart . . . and break clear away, once in a while, and climb a mountain or spend a week in the woods. Wash your spirit clean."
—John Muir

To Whom It May Concern,

In my class, we are learning about National Parks. I am learning about the Everglades.

    I am deeply concerned about us losing our National Parks because people may want to drill oil, build, cut the trees down, or fish. Things like loud oil drills, or people building, could take the peace away. Knowing that some people want to build there is a scary thought. Just to think of a park filled with cars is . . . really bad.

    I think the parks should be saved because they're such a wonderful place to escape from cities and enjoy nature. The parks should be left alone so people can still enjoy the world without buildings and cities. But if someone builds a city . . . well the point of the Parks is to enjoy nature . . . cars are not nature. Which is better: you going on vacation . . . or seeing cars and towns?

    My park, the Everglades, is a wonderful place. After learning about it sure, it seems like it's a ton of water and grass but really The Everglades are mostly water which is good if you want to see more of just that! Let's say you're on vacation in the Everglades running your hand in the streams of water, small animal noises and the sound of saw grass blowing in the wind fill your ear along with water rushing and the peaceful animals, it's the perfect vacation. But if someone is oil drilling there your vacation is interrupted by loud oil drills and cars.

    I hope you vote to save the parks. And if you have already voted to save the parks or are going to good! The parks are wonderful so protect them! Do what you can to save them!

Sincerely,

Natalia

History Inquiry on Westward Expansion in Fourth Grade

In any historical inquiry, one important focus is on understanding multiple perspectives. Resources include primary sources, video, images, online articles and images, maps, websites, and historical fiction.

Throughout a unit, questions that focus on history as a discipline include: *What really happened? How do we know? Is that the whole story? Is this true? Whose voice is missing? Whose perspectives inform our understanding?*

For the Westward Expansion unit, Karen introduces topic-specific essential questions and enduring understandings that come from district standards as well as bigger themes and issues, such as the causes and effects of human migration and settlement.

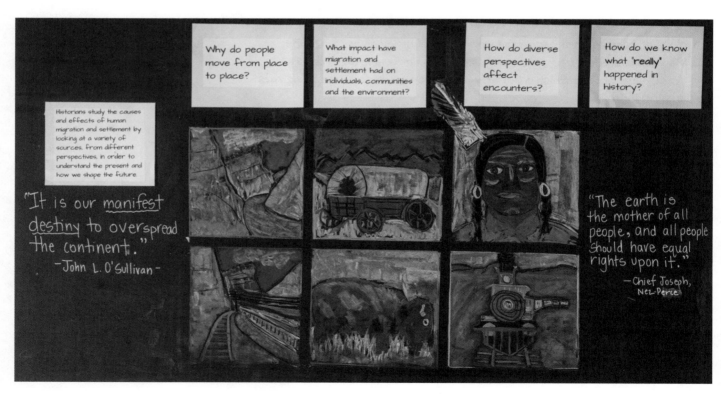

Two perspectives on Manifest Destiny are expressed through quotes and Karen's artistic images. This creation, with essential questions front and center in the classroom, becomes the focus of ongoing learning.

Enduring Understanding

Historians study the causes and effects of human migration and settlement by looking at a variety of sources, from different perspectives, to understand the present and how we shape the future.

Essential Questions

- Why do people move from place to place?
- How do diverse perspectives affect encounters?
- What impact have migration and settlement had on individuals, communities, and the environment?
- How do we know what "really" happened in history?

Students use comprehension strategies as tools to draw inferences about, question, summarize, and synthesize information from many sources related to Manifest Destiny. As their understanding builds over time, kids are able to take a more critical and evaluative stance toward sources and information.

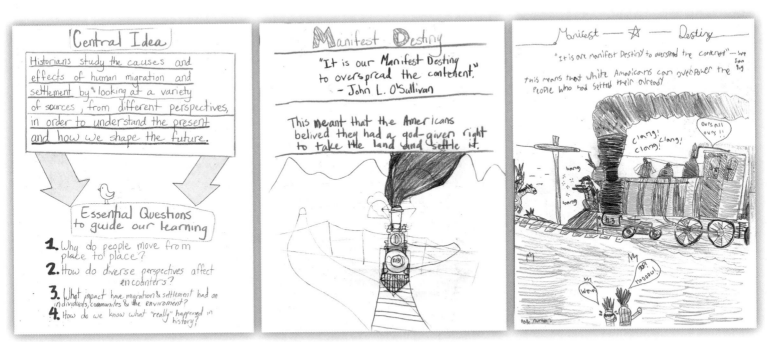

Kids record the enduring understanding and essential questions in their lesson books.

Kids have different initial interpretations of the idea of Manifest Destiny. They add to and refine their knowledge of this concept over time.

IMMERSE

Images express and provoke thinking. Photographs of Native Americans and covered wagons, evocative paintings of the journey west, and images of the building of the transcontinental railroad, among others, reflect the different perspectives kids will consider over the course of the unit.

Respond to images through a gallery walk. To build background knowledge about the big ideas of the unit, the class views and reacts to the image *American Progress* (by John Gast) together.

Viewing the image, kids consider these questions:

What do you notice?

What do you wonder?

What do you think is going on here?

What do you think the artist was trying to say?

Additional images are placed on large paper, roughly grouped by topic. Kids walk around to each group of images, observing and jotting thinking on the paper. Next, they read their peers' comments and add further thinking. After gathering to discuss and reflect, kids respond to the following prompts in their lesson books:

After viewing the images, I noticed . . .

I'm thinking that . . .

I'm wondering . . .

"Who is the woman? Why is she holding the telephone [telegraph] wire? Why is she floating over the land?"

"I notice buffalo running off into the distance, and the Native Americans look like they are fleeing. It's like they are being chased by the pioneers, a stagecoach, the railroad."

Consider different perspectives. Reflecting on the gallery walk, kids respond to these questions:

- How are different groups of people's experiences similar and different?
- Why is it important that we understand a variety of experiences and perspective?

To explore these questions further, kids view and respond to Chimamanda Ngozi Adichie's TED talk: "The Danger of a Single Story." Kids discuss and then reflect in their lesson books, using a gist/thinking scaffold.

Next, the class brainstorms a list of questions to push beyond a single story as students consider a person or group of people, historical or current. To experience misconceptions and stereotypes firsthand, they watch snippets of ways that Hollywood and the media have historically portrayed Native Americans.

Questions percolate:

- What do you think about this?
- How have peoples' stories been portrayed for them?
- What is the "white" perspective?

To broaden their knowledge with current-day perspectives, kids view a primary source: videos of Native Americans speaking up and out for themselves. Weaving in primary sources in this way wakes kids up to what they see and understand right now—so they can consider the question: What are we believing *right now* about history?

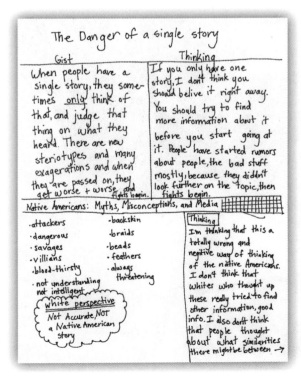

The Danger of a single story

Gist | Thinking
When people have a single story, they sometimes _only_ think of that, and judge that thing on what they heard. There are new steriotypes and many exagerations and when they are passed on, they get worse + worse, and fights begin. | If you only have one story, I don't think you should belive it right away. You should try to find more information about it before you start going at it. People have started rumors about people, the bad stuff mostly, because they didn't look further on the topic, then fights begin.

Native Americans: Myths, Misconceptions, and Media

- attackers
- dangerous
- savages
- villians
- blood-thirsty
- not understanding, not intelligent
  - white perspective
  - Not Accurate, NOT a Native American story

- backskin
- braids
- beads
- feathers
- always threatening

Thinking
I'm thinking that this a totally wrong and negitive way of thinking of the native Americans. I don't think that whites who thought up these really tried to find other information, good info. I also don't think that people thought about what similarities there might be between →

Pushing beyond a single Story

? Questions: ? ? ? ? ? ? ? ?
- Is this story Accurate? Is it true?
- What is true? What is good?
- How can I meet or experience this person/group "for real"?
- Is there more to this story?
- Who's Perspective? Who's telling the story?
- What are other perspectives?
- Where is this information coming from?
- How are we similar?

Native American Beyond the single story

- work hard for what they have
- earn money to pay for what they need
- are NOT given free money
- still honor their traditions
  - ~4.4 million in the US of A (from over 500 tribes)

They Are:
- youth leaders
- speakers
- teachers, professionals
- Not the stereotypes
- LIKE US
- play sports
- goes to school
- activists
- Elders
- film makers
- scholars
- fishermen
- veterans

Kids use the gist/thinking scaffold to reflect on the "danger of a single story." Examples from the ways in which Native Americans were portrayed in the media gets kids thinking about myths and misconceptions in the recent past.

Important questions lead to critical literacy. Kids come to understand multiple perspectives and develop a questioning and critical stance.

VIDEO CLIP

Read, analyze, and discuss historical sources to understand multiple perspectives.

Engage in Socratic seminar to deepen understanding.

INVESTIGATE/COALESCE

Investigate and coalesce happen in a cycle of learning and investigating. Students read a variety of sources and record notes and thinking, synthesizing their new learning.

Synthesize different perspectives. Over weeks, kids investigate what life was like and synthesize the perspectives of various groups of people: the pioneers, various Native American peoples, fur traders, gold seekers, among others. Students read primary sources, historical fiction, first-person accounts, textbook chapters, and view videos and images.

Throughout the study, students step into the shoes of those they are learning about, through drama and writing and working to make sense of different voices, perspectives, and stories. As they investigate, students pause to reflect and respond to the information and ideas through writing, discussion, and art.

Read and respond to historical fiction. When kids experience historical fiction, they break out of their immediate frame of reference and gain a more complete understanding of life in the past. Levstik and Barton (2001) suggest that historical narratives support an "informed and disciplined imaginative entry into events" so students build empathy for people long ago and far away.

Reading aloud the historical fiction chapter book *Hard Face Moon* by Nancy Oswald, a story of events surrounding Native Americans in the Colorado territory in the late 1800s, enables kids to experience characters from a Native perspective and build a deeper understanding of their way of life. When kids have "lived with" the characters in the story for some time, they come to care about them.

In their lesson books, kids respond to their reading of many different texts.

Examine different perspectives on the same issue. We return to the essential questions about different perspectives in relation to the idea of Manifest Destiny. Reading from primary sources and other informational texts, we learn about the acquisition of land to better understand the differing viewpoints. As students annotate and discuss articles, they unearth the deeper dynamics at work: the pioneer view that land can be owned and sold, that it is a commodity to be acquired versus the native view that the earth cannot be bought or sold, that it is something sacred—a gift from the creator.

This work prepares them for Socratic seminar. Viewing the projected image of an advertisement enticing settlers to move west, students discuss what they notice and what they think this advertisement means alongside whose perspective is represented and whose isn't.

To extend this learning, students view an NPR video about treaties. They record facts and thinking as they try to better understand treaties:

- What are they?
- What has happened the past?
- What am I thinking about this?

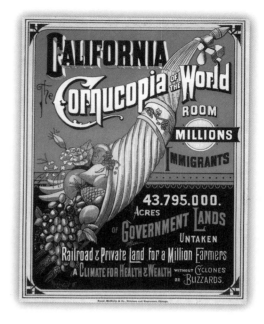

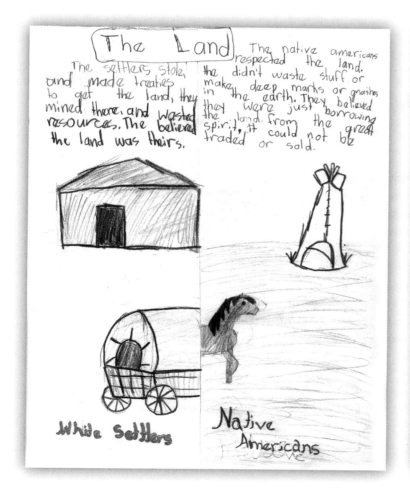

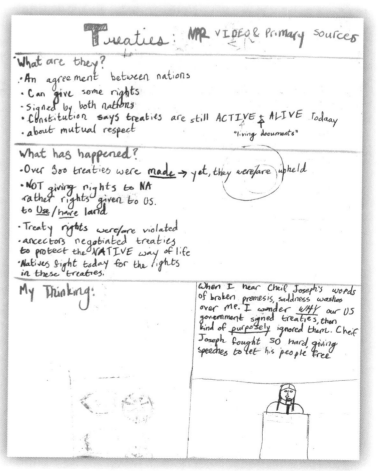

COALESCE/TAKE PUBLIC

Write historical fiction. Throughout the inquiry students create historical fiction flip journals, writing from the perspectives of both a Native American child and a pioneer child. Using historical information from their investigations in their writing helps solidify their learning. They enjoy naming themselves, imagining the journey west, envisioning themselves as part of a Native American tribe, experiencing the sights and sounds of lives long ago and far away. They are intensely engaged in this writing—crafting for themselves the drama and power of human experiences that are very different from their own.

> We are going to an English boarding school. I am in a wagon now, with Little Elk, Red Bird, Spotted Horse, Little Bluebell, Two Crows, Standing Tree, Sparkling Sea, and many more children. A mean woman and a mean man came to camp yesterday and took most of us (us=children). We all were torn out of our families' arms and put in these bumpy wagons. I am so sad. We will be in this school for a VERY long time . . . ACK! Now we are here! I'll be back to writing soon! Wow this place is BIG!

Children write from the perspective of a Native American child who has been sent to an Indian boarding school.

Kids take their historical fiction public, reacting to and enjoying each other's unique expression of the lives and times they have experienced.

> **River Crossing**
>
> June 21
>
> Dear Diary,
>
> Today we crossed the Platte River. It was far from pleasant but you could call it a big adventure, because it was. There was huge waves, rain, spooked cattle and noise, loud noise. Cadence crying, people shouting, waves crashing, and thunder booming. What an experience! We approached the river at a bad spot with no ferry so we had to take our wagon off its wheel bed and raft through the river. The currents were strong and I almost fell off. Twice! I hung on for dear life and squeezed my eyes shut. My heart beat fast. Finally, after what seemed like hours, I saw land. I paddled the wagon to shore and I scrambled to shore and I practically kissed the ground.

Writing as a pioneer child, this student describes a terrifying river crossing.

Respond to the essential questions through artistic expression. To synthesize their thinking across texts and experiences and respond to the essential questions framing the unit, kids create covers for their lesson books. Artistic expression offers kids a series of entry points into history, as well as being a way for them to synthesize their ideas and learning.

As they envision and create their covers, kids consider these questions:

- Reflecting on our learning, what lingers for you?
- What stands out for you about this time in history?
- What seem to be important ideas or themes of this time?
- What message might your art convey?

Kids have come to care about this time in history. Their imaginations take hold and their artwork expresses both different perspectives and complicated historical truths.

Wrap up by revisiting and discussing essential questions. Chart papers are posted around the room, each with one of the essential questions. Students move about the room in silence. They synthesize information and ideas they've accumulated over weeks of study and jot responses to each question. Then, they circulate again, responding to each other's thinking and discussing their insights.

What did kids learn from this history inquiry? Just as reading changes and shapes thinking, learning to read and think like historians changes how we view the past and the present. Although this unit was these students' first foray into a more formal study of history, they

- learned some tools for reading critically and beginning to think like historians
- realized the importance of accurate information, not for its own sake, but because it furthers historical understanding
- developed an awareness of and empathy for the different stories, events, and experiences of people in the past
- came to understand that there are many different historical truths and that reading and learning about different perspectives provides ways to get at those truths.

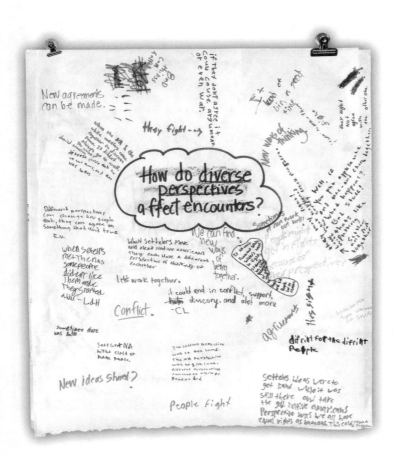

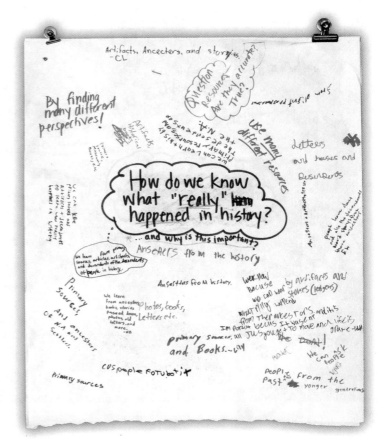

Inquiry Across the Curriculum

"Our lives begin to end the day we become silent about things that matter."

—Martin Luther King Jr.

In this chapter, fifth-grade teacher Karen Halverson shows what's possible when students have a solid foundation in inquiry-based learning. Inquiry becomes a way of life. Weaving together different disciplines in her workshop—in this case, literature, poetry, and social studies/history—Karen describes how reading, writing, discussion, personal reflection, and creative expression come to life when kids tackle issues involving social justice and historical and cultural perspectives both close to home and far away. She models every step in the inquiry process with her own thinking and creations. From Karen, we learn how kids can use the power of their own thinking, engagement with others, and the expression of their voices as vehicles for growth and change—both within and outside the classroom—over the course of a year.

Voice and Vote

August. Hiking in the hills above my Boulder home, I pondered the upcoming school year. Usually in the fifth grade, our social studies focused on Colonial times and the American Revolution, but this was an election year and I wanted to weave these current events into our historical study. At the same time, across our country, social justice issues seemed to be heated and illuminated more than they had been in decades. I wondered how to bring an awareness of issues into a classroom of ten- and eleven-year-olds. What was the common thread among these pieces? Voice, vote, rights, freedom. These words were arising again and again. These words would guide our year. We would begin with voice and the vote.

Essential questions surface:

In what ways do people express their voices?

How is a vote an expression of voice?

Who has or has not had the right to vote? Why?

In what ways have people expressed voice for the right to vote?

How has the expression of voice affected change?

An enduring understanding emerges: Throughout the history of our country, people have expressed their voices in pursuit of freedom, rights, and equality.

Be impeccable with your word. Speak with integrity. Say only what you mean. Avoid using the word to speak against yourself or to gossip about others. Use the power of your word in the direction of truth and love.

Our lives begin to end the day we become silent about things that matter.

I speak not for myself but for those without voice...those who have fought for their rights...their right to live in peace, their right to be treated with dignity, their right to equality of opportunity, their right to be educated.

When the whole world is silent, even one voice becomes powerful.
—Malala Yousafzai

Overview

Immerse

We consider the essential question: *In what ways do people express voice?* Kids work in small groups to read picture books about the many ways in which musicians, visual artists, activists of all kinds, sportspeople, poets, writers, political leaders, and many others express themselves and in doing so effect change. Kids then delve into the power of speech, the ways in which peoples' words impact historical and current events. Collecting and reflecting on ideas, thoughts, and quotes in their lesson books launches kids into the inquiry.

Investigate

Investigating the connection between voice and vote in current times leads to questions about voting rights and voting patterns, and how voting is an expression of voice, not to mention a foundation of democracy in the U.S. Kids research some of the historical struggles people experienced as they fought for the right to vote. Videos, articles, and books on women's suffrage of the late-nineteenth- and early-twentieth centuries and the civil rights movement in the 1960s make issues and events come alive. Students process all this through discussion and writing/drawing in their lesson books, synthesizing information using time lines, notes, and reflections.

Coalesce and Take Action

Students return to questions that have lingered throughout the inquiry and synthesize their learning from their dive into history. They create collages and craft essays that combine information and their carefully thought-out opinions. Finally, the students take action to bring their ideas and messages about voice and voting into the wider world.

Resources

A selection of videos and short texts—videos, infographics, historical images, websites, primary sources, and other informational excerpts and articles—provide content for students to view, read, annotate, and add to their lesson books. Zinn Education Project, Facing History and Ourselves, History.com, *Teaching Tolerance*, the *New York Times*, and *Newsela* are excellent places to begin. In addition, a classroom collection of informational books, purchased or borrowed from the library, is essential. For this inquiry, we use books related to women's suffrage, voting rights in general and in the 1960s, and U.S. elections.

A collection of picture books supports interactive read-alouds, small-group work, and student reading throughout the inquiry. Chosen for their powerful messages about voice or the vote, these picture books provide a narrative thread to our inquiry: *Malala, A Brave Girl from Pakistan*; *Emmanuel's Dream: The True Story of Emmanuel Ofosu Yeboah*; *When Marian Sang*; *Trombone Shorty*; *Brave Girl: Clara and the Shirtwaist Makers' Strike of 1909*; *Maybe Something Beautiful: How Art Transformed a Neighborhood*; *When the Beat Was Born: DJ Cool Herc and the Creation of Hip-Hop*; *Nasreen's Secret School: A True Story from Afghanistan*; *Heart on Fire: Susan B. Anthony Votes for President*; *Elizabeth Leads the Way: Elizabeth Cady Stanton and the Right to Vote*; *Lillian's Right to Vote: A Celebration of the Voting Rights Act of 1965*; and *Granddaddy's Turn: A Journey to the Ballot Box*.

Throughout the year, kids keep several notebooks simultaneously. In addition to their reader's and writer's notebooks—for, obviously, reading and writing—they use their lesson books as their primary place to hold student learning in content areas, beginning a new one each time we start a new inquiry in social studies or science. Typically, these are bound notebooks with both blank and lined paper, usually only thirty-two pages, allowing the notebook to be focused on the most essential components of the inquiry, eventually becoming a body of work, a record of the journey. The contents comprise essential questions, enduring understandings, student research, thinking, reflections, diagrams, artwork, writing, and other elements of significance to the inquiry. This is also a place where beauty and craftsmanship in one's work is paramount.

With time lines, posters, collages, and lesson book cover art woven into this inquiry, art materials are as much a classroom staple as pens and pencils. Large drawing paper, poster board, watercolor paper, collage boards, a collection of used and donated magazines, paints, poster markers, and Mod Podge make a good beginning collection.

"Women expressed their voices through protest. They fought for their rights to vote by trying to vote and showing up with signs in front of the White House. After 72 years of hard fighting, they won the right to vote! My mind lingers with the fact that people opposed to women's suffrage were so unfair. They don't care that women had been fighting for over 70 years. I wonder what the mindset of those people were (was)."

Gist and Thinking for a video about women's suffrage (*right page*). On the left, a student illustration and reflection on the question: From your learning on women's suffrage, what lingers and why?

What Is Voice?

IMMERSE

■ Explore the concept of *voice*.

"Your voice matters" is written in large, white letters on the board in the back of the room. Surrounding this message are the rough chalk-drawn images of some who have expressed their voices in powerful ways: Malala Yousafzai, Marian Anderson, Elizabeth Cady Stanton, Clara Lemlich, Trombone Shorty, and Langston Hughes. Alongside the chalkboard are several quotes on voice. These voices will speak as mentors, guiding historical and current event studies, encouraging questions, and uncovering the voices and messages within ourselves that most fervently desire expression.

"In what ways do people express voice?" Fifth graders turn and talk, discussing the question. Speeches, emails, newspapers, music, poetry, books. Expanding the idea of artistic expression as voice, students offer dance, instrumental music, sculpture, and other forms of visual art, which leads to signs, which leads to protest. Suddenly the room erupts into an enthusiastic shoutout: signs, banners, body painting, clothing, marches, bodies as blockade, work strikes, hunger strikes, film, social media. This is relevant and they want to be a part of it.

> "I speak not for myself but for those without voice . . . those who fought for their rights . . . their right to live in peace, their right to be treated with dignity, their right to equality of opportunity, their right to be educated."
>
> —Malala Yousafzai

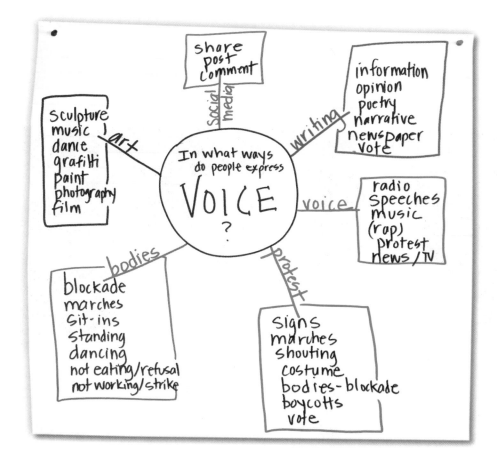

Classroom chart holds student thinking about voice.

Expanding the concept of voice in picture book groups. From here, we move this enthusiasm into small-group work, each group reading and responding to a different picture book. Their mission: to learn more about individuals who have expressed their voices in various ways to effect change and to understand why people are willing to speak out and what risks are they willing to take.

Four questions guide the reading:

- How is voice expressed?
- What is the message?
- Why is this message important?
- How did this expression of voice affect others/bring about change?

We model with a read-aloud of the picture book *Malala, A Brave Girl from Pakistan*, and we discuss our thinking and responses to these questions. Students form groups, select a picture book from our collection, and record their responses to the four questions.

As they read aloud and discuss the books, students notice the risks people have taken to speak out and take a stand, and then are awed that such change could be effected by such courage and determination.

Kids who read about Emmanuel, the one-legged cyclist; Trombone Shorty, the New Orleans musician; Clara Lemlich, the labor activist; or singer Marian Anderson get right to the heart of each person's life.

Student 1 I can't imagine biking that far with one leg! He was determined to show that his disability didn't matter.

Student 2 Well, Trombone Shorty made a new kind of music that people liked, but is there a message he is trying to express?

Student 3 Wow. Those workers were treated so unfairly! That just seems so wrong.

Student 4 I didn't realize black people weren't allowed to do so many things. Marian [Anderson] must have been nervous singing to such a large audience!

Reflecting on voice. Each group presents its learning to the class. We are beginning to understand the importance of voice, the myriad of ways one can express it, and how this can affect change in one's life and community, and even across a country. Later that day, students freewrite, bringing these ideas into their personal, everyday, lives: *Write about a time when you used your voice in a powerful way. How did that feel? What change did it effect?*

Studying speech as an expression of voice. The next day, to expand students' background knowledge and to give them a deeper sense of the power words have to affect others, we read the article "The Power of Speech" (from National Geographic's *Ladders*), which takes an historical look at the purpose and impact of speeches given by well-known orators; for example, John F. Kennedy, Martin Luther King Jr., Sojourner Truth, and Sandra Day O'Connor. With a copy of the article on the doc camera, we annotate the gist and thinking as we work through the text.

Kids come to understand different purposes for speeches and how they can powerfully affect others, call for change, and bring people together. Students break into groups to continue to annotate specific sections of the article. They learn about speeches that have profoundly affected others and have lingered in history. Read. Jot. Discuss. We jigsaw to share our learning and insight.

Students' homework that evening is to gather a few quotes on voice and speaking out that inspire them. The next day in class, students buzz about the quotes they have collected. Eagerly, they cut and paste or copy them into their lesson books. While some students have two or three quotes, others collected a pageful. This page becomes a collecting space for added inspiration as we continue our inquiry.

\Voice quotes/

"Our lives begin to end the day we become silent about things that matter." - Martin Luther King Jr.

"Don't raise your voice, improve your arguement."

"Don't try to figure out what other people want to hear from you; figure out what you have to say. -Barbara Kingsolver

"My vote is my voice... and the voice of all who struggled so that I may have a voice." -Lydia C. Obas

INVESTIGATE

■ Create essential questions for voting.

An election year offers a unique energy and perspective to the exploration of voice. Our essential questions invite voices into our conversations, not only current voices urging the American people to vote, but also the historical voices of American people who have not had that right. We wonder:

- How is a vote an expression of voice?
- Who has or has not had the right to vote? Why?
- What have people been willing to do to get that right?
- How has the expression of voice affected change?

This part of the inquiry leads us to seek understanding of how our government and electoral system work; the agreements, documents, and individuals that founded our country; the perspectives and experiences of diverse groups of people; what it means to have equal rights; and the importance that voice plays throughout all of these.

At the rug, we begin by discussing the questions that launched this inquiry: *How is vote an expression of voice? Why is it important? How have individuals used their voice?* We consider small votes that might determine whether our class has extra reading or recess time or how their family might spend the day. We talk about the importance of their voice as a vote.

Our conversation expands to consider voting for local issues, for members of Congress as well as for President. What happens if people don't vote? Why might people not vote? How might this change things? To help us consider these questions from a more informed position, we view and annotate an infographic entitled "Who Actually Votes in America?" that shows the breakdown of people by age and whether or not they voted in the 2008 election.

At table groups, students discuss what they notice, then mark surprises, jot questions, and record their thinking. One statistic that lingers strongly in everyone's mind is the fact that voter turnout increases with age. "Wow! The eighteen- to twenty-four-year-olds have the lowest voter turnout!" Why might that be so? While they can imagine possible reasons, they are actually incredulous that anyone, especially young people, wouldn't want to have a say, as these fifth graders are bucking to have the opportunity to vote.

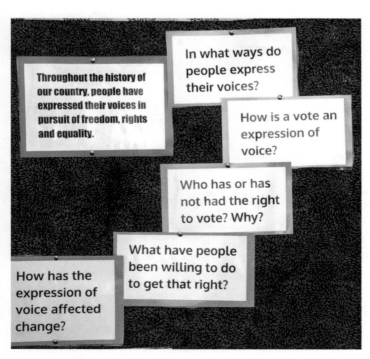

Grabbing our attention is a percentage breakdown of the most common reasons why people don't vote: too busy; sick or disabled; not interested; don't like the campaign, candidates, or issues. "What?!" Students eagerly argue against most of these reasons based on the idea that voting is a right, an opportunity, a responsibility.

We view two videos that encourage everyone to exercise their right to vote. In one video, a young woman speaks more directly to the youngest of voters, emphasizing the potential impact of these young voices. In the other video, an array of well-known faces join together to get out the vote, highlighting the importance of this right.

Creating persuasive messages. With this inspired vision, students return to their lesson books: "What is your message to voters? What would you most like to say?" After several minutes of writing, students highlight essential words and persuasive phrases, distilling and clarifying the essence of their message.

With these messages in mind, we consider the mash-up of word and art as a vehicle for expression. We consider the election and the importance of the vote. We reconsider the all the reasons Americans have for not voting. And we design drafts of artistic word messages for signs that later in the inquiry we will stake on the front lawn of our campus, signs that we hope will encourage all passersby to get out and vote! Fifth graders may be too young to vote, but they are not too young to have a voice.

■ Trace voice and voting in history.

Although students have a sprinkling of information suggesting everyone has not always had the right to vote, they have no idea how immense and hard fought the battle for the vote has been in American history. Through the lens of history, we will trace the inquiry theme of voice and voting.

Creating time lines. Reading, annotating, and discussing articles that highlight events in America's voting history, students touch upon the inequalities that have existed between groups of people. To help students organize and keep track of important events, individuals, and amendments, they each create a labeled and illustrated time line that becomes a working document for new information throughout our learning. To deepen our inquiry, we focus on two primary voting rights movements: women's suffrage and the voting rights marches of 1965.

Investigating the women's suffrage movement. We read aloud *Heart on Fire: Susan B. Anthony Votes for President*, a story of how Anthony voted in the 1872 presidential election, then was arrested, tried, found guilty, and fined. The case helped bring attention to the suffragist movement. Although women did not gain the right to vote until 1920, this book demonstrates how Anthony, Elizabeth Cady Stanton, and other early activists were tireless in their efforts. Students are shocked not only by the treatment of Susan B. Anthony but also the treatment of all women at the time. Why were women denied the right to vote?

Reading excerpts from *The Split History of the Women's Suffrage Movement*, we learn more about the perspective that many people had at that time: that women were not considered equals in body or mind, and therefore should not have the right to vote. We view images of women out in their communities,

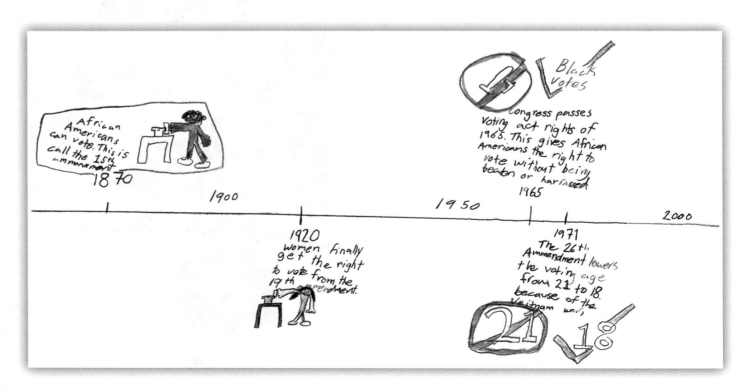

expressing their voices and inviting others to join their movement alongside images of those working to suppress this movement. With percolating questions, students annotate their thinking alongside these texts and images.

Students move into small groups with excerpted text from *Created Equal*, which details the events and the leaders of the women's suffrage movement, from the first Women's Rights Convention in 1948 to the passage of the Nineteenth Amendment in 1920. Reading, discussing, and annotating their thinking, students learn about the steadfast efforts and courageous risks suffragists were willing to take to have their voices heard.

Viewing and reacting to a film on the struggle for voting rights. Next, we turn our attention to Selma and the Voting Rights March of 1965. We begin by reading an excerpt from the book *Turning 15 on the Road to Freedom* projected on the document camera. The author, who turned fifteen years old while marching to Selma for the right to vote, describes the inequality, fear, and injustice of that time as well as the courage and determination that it took to stand up, to march, to speak out against such injustice. As a class, we read, wonder, turn and talk, jot our thinking.

We view the film *Selma: The Bridge to the Ballot*, a powerful video available from Teaching Tolerance. Although it contains strong images from the protests in Alabama, students witness the truth of the injustices of that time as well as the absolute determination of the African Americans, and others who supported them, to stand up for justice and equality. Students realize anew how valuable this right to vote is and the risks that were taken to give this right to every American citizen.

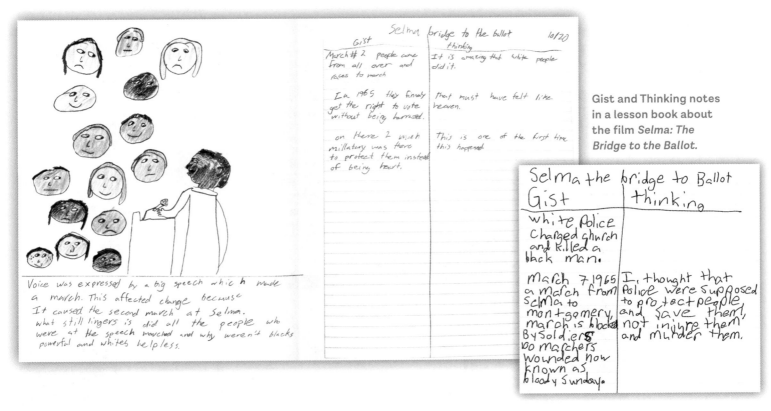

Gist and Thinking notes in a lesson book about the film *Selma: The Bridge to the Ballot.*

Just as they would when reading a text, students annotate their thinking when viewing a film. They create two-column note-taking pages, labeled *Gist* and *Thinking*, and take notes as we view the film (see p. 221). Overall, the film emphasizes the courage, hope, and determination shown throughout the marches. Yet, as uplifting as these themes are, questions about our history as a nation surface and lead to further study:

Why has there been separation between groups of people?

Why has there been superiority of one group over another?

Who has had the power? Who has not? Why?

What was it like when our country began? Has our country included all voices? Is it fair? What is a democracy?

Do we really have one?

WE THE PEOPLE—who is that, really?

We list these burning questions on chart paper and post them in front of the room so that we may come back to them again and again.

■ Create a tableau.

Drama is a powerful way to help students grasp another's perspective and to deepen their understanding. Students form groups of five to seven. Each group draws a slip of paper with either "women's suffrage" or "Selma" written on it, determining the focus for their drama. The task is to create a tableau (a frozen scene) that shows people expressing their voices to effect change during that

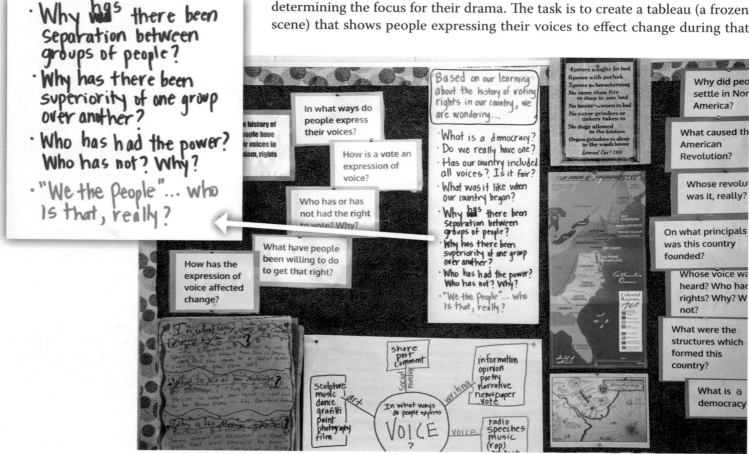

time in history. Students have twenty minutes to assign roles and plan their tableaux, then return for presentations. While the audience closes their eyes, one group moves into their tableau at the front of the room. When they are ready, the audience opens their eyes to view and understand what might be happening in the tableau. As a tableau member's shoulder is tapped, each in turn speaks from his or her point of view as that person in history. After each person has spoken, the group relaxes back into fifth graders.

After viewing all tableaux, students turn to their lesson books to synthesize their learning and answer questions: What lingers in your mind from the women's suffrage movement? What stands out for you from the Selma to Montgomery marches? Students must create an illustration or symbolic drawing to represent their answers to these questions. Leaving space at the bottom of the page for a paragraph of text, students write a response to these questions: How was voice expressed? What change did it effect? What lingers most in your mind?

Students synthesize their learning in response to questions.

"Voice was expressed by protesting, by showing up and having signs and using their voice. This affected the amendment happening in the women's favor. What lingers in my mind is that men just thought that women had mental issues, they thought they would make bad judgments when they voted."

> *"Coming to voice is coming to power—daring to make life in words— daring to be heard."*
>
> —bell hooks

COALESCE/TAKE PUBLIC

■ Write an essay and create a collage.

The questions we have considered throughout the inquiry thus far have engaged students' minds but also their hearts. These are topics that matter to them and the time is ripe for students to extend their thinking to distill the information, the experiences, their emotions, and their questions by creating collages and writing essays. Using freewrites to unload our thinking, we freewrite on a number of topics and questions we have tackled through our inquiry. Kids notice what is most weighty, what is most pertinent, what wants to be expressed. After sharing their freewrites with one another, they choose an idea they are willing to linger with and delve into more deeply.

To further explore their chosen topics, students prepare to create collages. Art connects students deeply with ideas and opens them to new ways of seeing. They must first define the message or statement they would like to make through their art and writing.

Then, students work to gather:

- 2–3 relevant quotes
- 2–3 powerful, related facts or statistics
- 2–3 essential words
- 3–4 images, photographs, or illustrations.

"Voice, Vote, Equality and Freedom"
End of Unit Collage-Writing Project
Art Piece Guidelines

Audience: classmates, families, students
Purpose: to inform, to make a statement or send a message

1. Choose the focus for your project. This may be any event (Selma March), concept (Women's Equality), big idea (All Voices Matter), or essential question (Whose revolution was it, really?) from our weeks of learning.

Focus:

_____

2. What is the question, message, central idea or statement you would like to make through your art and your writing? Keep this in mind as you collect for your collage.

Message:

_____

_____

3. Collect in a google doc in your google drive:
   - 2-3 relevant quotes
   - 2-3 powerful, related facts or statistics
   - 2-3 essential words
   - 3-4 images, photographs or illustrations

4. Everything must be printed by Friday morning. BE PREPARED! We are making our collages Friday afternoon.

Alongside this work, students begin the essay process. Mentor texts lead the way, always. Knowing these essays and collages will be published in a class magazine, we use Leonard Pitts Jr., journalist, columnist, and word weaver extraordinaire, as our guide. We read several of his pieces and share our initial feelings, connections, and responses to his ideas. We consider: *What do we notice about voice? What do we notice about the structure of this piece? What do we notice about the craft?*

Soon, collections of quotes, facts, and power words spread over desks. Magazines sprawl throughout the room. Scissors, Mod Podge, and collage boards add to the chaos. It's collage assembly day. Piece by piece, messages of equality, voice, rights, and the vote emerge. As they cut and arrange, glue and gloss, students revise and clarify their thinking, preparing them to revise and clarify their writing.

Students continue to work on their essays, weaving the quotes and facts from their collages as integral threads throughout their pieces. Together, we create a rubric for our writing based on our noticings from the mentor texts. We agree on which elements are must-haves—an introduction, specific examples, personal opinion—in our essays and which are might-haves, stand-alone sentences, repetition, humor. This rubric guides revision. Students confer with each other, reread, revise, and in the process, discover the power in expressing something that matters to them.

Eventually, the students' final pieces head to the print shop. We wait, eagerly, until one day the box arrives. We tear it open. Twenty-eight smooth and glossy magazines appear, beautifully bound and in color. Delighted, we spend the next long while drifting through the words and images we have crafted and designed, each other's voices proclaiming our places in the world between pages.

This excerpt from an essay accompanies a collage created about voice.

VOICE, VOTE,

Your voice matters.

FREEDOM AND EQUALITY

When a Voice Is Not Heard

"At what price do we pay to be heard?"

Some people ask, "Why doesn't anyone speak up for the African Americans?" or "Why doesn't anyone stand up for what is right?" Most people are too scared to stand up to the authorities, but the people who do get shut down. Fear is overpowering bravery.

Violence is not a voice. It is an action. A horrible action. It is an action that blocks the real voice from escaping its barriers. We tied ropes around their necks and arms, giving them rope burns that sting. The police trapped them in cells with one locked door and no windows and it was horribly hot in there. The African Americans still marched for their right to vote, and a vote is a voice and more than ever they wanted a voice. The African Americans sang, they danced, and they prayed and with that they marched with proud faces. They overcame the violence and this time they were stronger. They still had fear in their eyes but they were together, fighting for what they thought was right."

■ March to take action.

Now the kids have a much deeper understanding of the struggle for voting rights throughout American history—past and present. They know that voting is a right and that people fought and even died to have this right. And they have learned that not everyone exercises this precious right to vote. With enthusiasm and conviction, students make artistic posters from the rough drafts of persuasive get-out-the-vote messages they created earlier, mount their signs on stakes, and pound the stakes into the ground outside the school. As the last sign is staked firmly into the ground, we hope. We hope the wind or mischievous neighbors won't take away the signs overnight. We hope passersby will be impacted by our messages. And then we think of the youngest population of voters, only six blocks away on the University of Colorado campus . . . and an idea is born.

Still humming with the energy of the marches of 1965, we decide to march. We will take our signs from the schoolyard and march onto the CU campus, encouraging these college voters to take action. Since fifth graders cannot vote, they will use their voices to speak out to others, to get out the vote.

The excitement is contagious! Parents eagerly volunteer. Colorado Public Radio (CPR) promptly commits their team. Students double-staple their signs and nervously consider possible interview questions. The morning of our march, we gather to discuss how we want to express our message. What will that look like? What will that sound like? We reflect on recent presidential debate clips, which we had analyzed for passive, assertive, and aggressive behavior. We consider how each of those behaviors had affected us as an audience and how the behaviors had affected the speakers' messages. Together, we agree that we want

to be assertive but not aggressive. That we want to shout out our messages of encouragement, but do not want to turn listeners away with any negativity. We also consider how our verbal silence could amplify the message of our artistic-word pieces. With excitement in our legs and lungs, and our signs held high, we set out the door of our classroom.

"V-O-T-E, Vote!!" students chant as we march onto campus. College students turn, watch, listen, smile. Some shout out, "I voted!" which elicits cheers from the fifth-grade marchers. Past dorms and classrooms, we march, chant, and shout our message that all voices matter, vote, it's your right! As we lounge on the quad for a snack break, college students wander over to encourage these young marchers, "Did you make these signs yourselves? They look great! Keep marching. What you are doing is cool . . . important." In between bites of apples and sandwiches, students offer their insights to CPR reporter Jenny Brundin. They eagerly express their thinking. They want to be heard!

> *"Humans aren't as good as we should be in our capacity to empathize with feelings and thoughts of others, be they humans or other animals on Earth. So maybe part of our formal education should be training in empathy. Imagine how different the world would be if, in fact, that were 'reading, writing, arithmetic, and empathy.'"*
>
> —Neil DeGrasse Tyson

Hours later, after a final march through campus, we take the public bus rather than walk home. Exhausted from the day's mission, students rest quietly, still holding their signs, while curious passengers smile and take phone videos of the weary messengers. As we step off the bus and back into our classroom, it feels as if we have been on a long journey, a journey that has changed us. Together, we have felt the passionate spark of conviction and allowed it to move us into real-world action. Days later the story airs on CPR (https://bit.ly/2enUENA). Then, National Public Radio decides to air the story the day before the election! These students' voices are heard by an audience far greater than anything we had ever imagined. Emails roll in about the positive, uplifting impact of their message, including at least one story of a nonvoter whose mind was changed and decided to vote.

What a perfect place from which to launch our next history unit, the road to revolution—the American Revolution of 1776, that is.

Slamming for Social Justice

April. Considering how we will spend our last eight weeks together, I want to offer an experience that harnesses all of these energies, expands students' awareness of self and current issues in the world, and creates a platform of bravery from which to fly—all the while remembering the message written boldly on our blackboard, "Your voice matters!" I want students to make connections between what they value most at this point in their lives and issues of the big world out there, encouraging them to imagine what action they and their communities could take, even in small ways, to make the world a better place. The key here is building empathy, moving beyond the facts, and imagining life in another's shoes. For this is the true purpose of what we do each day in the classroom. Is it not?

Social justice and environmental issues seem like the perfect place to start. These issues comprise a vast and significant field in our society. Social justice issues occur globally, nationally, regionally, locally, and within groups. These issues are a result of unequal wealth and resource distribution, unfair treatment of individuals with differing traits—race, culture, sexual orientation, religion, and so on—and laws that support segregation. We will immerse ourselves in the issues, raise questions, and investigate further, unite our heads and hearts around the content, and take our voices public. Envisioning our work, essential questions pour forth:

> "Coming to voice is coming to power—daring to make life in words—daring to be heard."
>
> —bell hooks—
>
> Karen

"I Can't Keep Quiet"

Big idea The quest for social justice is a never ending struggle in our nation and world. We must understand this struggle and make decisions about whether to be involved in it.

Guiding Questions!
- What is justice?
- What is social justice?
- What are the social justice and environmental issues in our nation & world?
- What causes these issues?
- What are the effects of these issues?
- Whose voices are heard? are not heard?
- What do we value?
- What do we stand for?
- What is our responsibility?
- How can our voices be heard?
- How are our lives connected to and limited by society?

Throughout the inquiry Karen models responses, notes, artistic expression, and reflections in her own lesson book. She writes and creates along with the students.

What is justice? Social justice?

What social justice and environmental issues do we notice in the world?

What causes these issues? What are the effects of these issues?

What do we value? What is our responsibility? What do we stand for?

How can we take action? How can our voices be heard?

How are our lives connected to and limited by society?

Inspired by Bill Bigelow and his work with Rethinking Schools, our enduring understanding takes form: The quest for social justice is a never-ending struggle in our nation and world. We must make decisions about whether to be involved in it.

Overview

This end-of-year inquiry spans seven weeks and includes a series of weeklong mini-inquiries. Throughout, students will create a portfolio of poetry and art expressing their personal identity, core values, and deepest learnings, alongside their wonderings, their attempts to step into another's shoes, and their voices standing for good in the world. From this work, students choose an issue of importance to them to fuel their final creations and performances.

Week 1: Exploring Identity

Before we can dive into issues and consider life from another's perspective, we must first consider our own. We spend the first week defining ourselves, creating life maps, heart maps, and world maps to animate this exploration.

Weeks 2–5: Investigating Issues

Kids explore four key mini-inquiries, one per week, drawn from our year's learning. Topics that have captured kids' interest during our history units and sparked discussion of current events include:

- Week 2: The Women's Movement/Feminism
- Week 3: LGBTQ Issues and Rights
- Week 4: Othering—Immigration, Race, Religion
- Week 5: Environment—Threats and Changes

Note: Week 5 appears on p. 238 as an example of a one-week inquiry.

Weeks 6–7: Creating and Performing Poetry

This series of inquiries culminates in a poetry slam performance for our peers and families, the ultimate invitation to stand, with courage, determination, and bravery, in one's voice and to speak out for what matters.

Resources

Text collections are at the core of our learning. A shared read-aloud—*Sylvia and Aki* by Winifred Conkling—is a story about two families, one Japanese-American and the other Mexican whose lives intersect in the 1940s Southern California. This book launches our conversation around social justice issues. Collections of poetry mentor texts and slam mentor videos inform our writing and speaking. Fiction book sets—four to six copies of several novels—invite small groups of readers to consider aspects of social justice or environmental issues: *The Breadwinner, Journey of the Sparrows, Gracefully Grayson, One Crazy Summer, Red Berries-White Clouds-Blue Sky, Operation Redwood, Weedflower, Esperañza Rising, Inside Out and Back Again, In the Year of the Boar and Jackie Robinson.* Scrolling through the online news provides digital resources for social justice and environmental issues. Articles, YouTube videos, and websites provide context for class discussion as well as for independent exploration.

The lesson books continue to be places to hold kids' ongoing thinking, their responses and questions, notes on videos and readings, and their own original poetry accompanied by artistic creations. Identity work, reflections on social justice issues, and different forms of poetry offer rich opportunities for thoughtful reflection and creative response. With published poetry and art pieces as significant components of this inquiry, materials and art supplies are critical for students' creative work.

And so, we begin. . . .

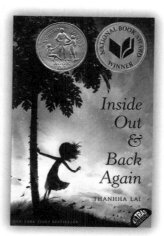

Week 1: Exploring Identity

As our inquiry into social justice begins, we spend a week on identity, exploring these questions as an avenue into social issues in weeks 2–5.

- What stories and circumstances have brought me to this moment in my life?
- What are my core values?
- What guides my words, actions, and choices? How do I generally view the world? What do I see? What do I feel and think about what I see?
- What am I compelled to do about what I see?

Kids have pondered these questions all year long. To delve into these questions now, we create three maps: a life map, a heart map, and a world map. These exploratory tools invite students to investigate "Who am I now?" playfully, yet meaningfully. Alongside all our map work, we expand our thinking through table shares, turn and talks, and freewrites in our notebooks. We ask ourselves and each other, "What feels important? How does that make me feel? What questions arise? What lingers?" And of course, to synthesize all that comes up within this part of the inquiry, we write poetry and create art.

■ Define ourselves with life maps.

Through this map, students consider people, places, and life moments and lessons that have shaped them. On blank paper, they draw a line to represent their life, from birth to present, which approximates the ups and downs of their life. Then they add, in words, symbols, or images to mark significant features of their journey:

- people: family, friends, enemies
- places: homes, secret spaces, outdoor spaces
- things: pets, treasures
- moments/events: births, deaths, celebrations, losses, accomplishments, failures, firsts, life lessons.

Knowing where we come from and understanding our own stories can help us understand others.'

> *"Every social justice movement that I know of has come out of people sitting in small groups, telling their life stories, and discovering that other people have shared similar experiences."*
>
> —Gloria Steinem

Sharing objects. Dropping deeper into stories and how they inform our identities, students bring three objects to school that represent something about who they are, looking for the deeper meaning in any object they choose. Rather than bringing a rock because they like rocks, they may realize that the rock actually represents a deep connection to the earth. Sitting in circle, with objects placed before them, students take turns sharing.

● What did you bring and why?
● What stories belong with these objects?
● What do these objects represent about your identity? What do they say about who you are?

Even though these students have been together in school for years, their identities are ever shifting. As they share, connections are realized, and we see the similarities in our stories.

> "I try to find the core values that are so fundamental that they transcend ethnic identity. That doesn't mean I run from it. I embrace African American culture and I love it, but it is a part of a human identity. So I'm always trying to make a larger human statement."
>
> —Wynton Marsalis

Freewriting to respond to a video. We view a video of a powerful spoken word piece by Prince Ea, "I am NOT black, you are NOT white," which asks us to consider the idea of labels and where they come from, expanding our perspective of ourselves and others and societies' role in that labeling. A freewrite and class discussion generates yet another a list of questions:

- How do labels begin? Why do we label each other?
- Who would you be if the world never gave you a label?
- How do labels tell stories?
- How do labels divide us? How can we remove labels?
- What is the truth about labels?

■ Reflect our values with heart maps.

Working with Georgia Heard's *Heart Maps* (2016), students consider their own core values. Here, we are pushing students to feel more deeply into personal values, deeper than the generally accepted answers of valuing love or kindness or fairness along with all other "positive" values. Although those may be somewhat true for any individual, asking students to consider which core values guide them each day, inform their actions and words, and help determine their choices may help reveal what matters most to them.

I Am From

I am from dust covered workshops and wild weather
Rocket parks and bookshelfs
I am from lonely basketball courts
And homegrown peaches
The apple tree
The raspberry bush
This is where I'm from.

I am from exotic birds and pesky squirrels
Spring rolls and sloping hills
I am from crispy bacon
And dancing and shakin'.

I am from "Brush your teeth" and
"Don't give me a hassle!"
Snow forts and fish tacos

I am from grandparents and cousins
Aunts and uncles
Wet kisses and calloused hands.

I am from broken arms and pokey bushes
The big bad wolf and plenty of wishes.
I am from my childhood
My home
My memories
My photos

I am from where I came from
And that will never change.

On blank paper, students draw a large outline of a heart. As a class, we brainstorm possible core value words such as honesty, justice, creativity, love, curiosity, humility, balance, kindness. Using words, symbols, or images, students fill the heart with words that resonate most powerfully for them. Knowing what we value most allows us to look for those qualities, or the lack of them, out in the world. Clarity of these values may help create common ground between people or groups of people. Driven by core values, we choose how and where we will speak up, stand up, or take action in the world.

Creating poetry and art. With life stories and heart values awakened, students are ready to craft their first poem. George Ella Lyon's poem, "Where I Come From" is our mentor text. We read the poem aloud, just to hear it, and then reread, to notice our feelings and connections. Finally, kids notice the voice, structure, and craft. We make lists, paralleling the types of items in the poem. Kids dive into drafting "Where I Come From" poems of their own.

Students begin "identity" art pieces. Just as we use mentor texts for writing, we also study mentor pieces for students' artwork. We often look at several images, printed or online, alongside the art tools we'll be using. Although students are *not* attempting to re-create any mentor art piece, they are given some inspiration and beginning vision to work with in creating original art of their own. (Never do we want to have twenty-eight matching turkeys, or any other matching artwork, hanging in the hall!) Through writing and art, a dance of reflection and expression occurs, driving their learning deeper.

> *"Revolution is something that actually starts in individual hearts."*
> —Bill Viola

■ Capture our view of the world with world maps.

Through this map, students awaken their awareness of issues in society, creating a bridge to our upcoming work. They turn their attention away from themselves for a moment and look out into the world.

- What do you see?
- What do you hear?
- What concerns you?
- What feels unjust?
- What feels hopeful?
- What needs our attention?

Using an outline or a sketch of a world map, kids fill in their knowledge of challenges people face around the world. They share their observations with their table groups. These maps help us better understand where we all stand in our awareness of the world and guide us all in our inquiries ahead.

In this first week, we have not only laid the foundation for our inquiry into social justice and environmental issues, but also moved through a dance of immerse, investigate, and coalesce created by reading, viewing, writing, discussing, moving, questioning, and creating. The integration of workshops through the inquiry framework offers a rich and dynamic learning environment through which any content can be explored.

"Until the great mass of the people shall be filled with the sense of responsibility for each other's welfare, social justice can never be attained."

—Helen Keller

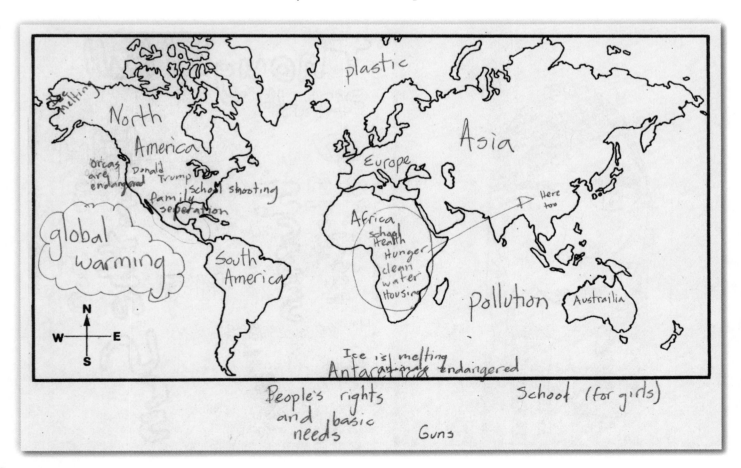

IMMERSE/INVESTIGATE/COALESCE

Weeks 2–5: Investigating Issues

In each of weeks 2–5, we enter a new mini-inquiry under the larger umbrella of social justice. Together as class we decide on social issues we want to explore each week. These mini-inquiries follow a similar sequence:

We spend several sessions—for example, on Monday and Tuesday of each week—engaged with our chosen issue: interacting with picture book and novel read-alouds, reading and annotating articles, viewing and discussing video, and reading and analyzing poetry. Exploring these resources for starters, we quickly move into investigation, gathering information and keeping track of our observations and questions through our favorite forms of *Gist/Thinking* double-column notes or *Facts/Issue/Thinking* triple-column notes on charts and in our lesson books.

Discussion is constant: turn and talk, table share, dyad, triad, circle within a circle, whole-class discussion, and Socratic seminar. Even as we continue to investigate, we begin to synthesize learning, which takes the remainder of the week. Kids write to discover their thinking through power-writes, responding to text, reflecting on questions. Frequently, we step into another's shoes through drama, creating tableaux, or frozen scenes, inspired by information gathered. From these still life snapshots, students speak from another's perspective, cultivating empathy for others.

Alongside our work with issues, we inquire into the nature of slam poetry in preparation for our final projects. Throughout the year, kids have responded to a variety of topics with poetry, a natural expression of voice, so slam poetry is a logical next step. Each week, we watch video of slam artists performing, seeking to understand this form. What is it like? How does it feel? What do we notice? We chart lists of our observations, referring to them again and again as we create our own pieces.

Our inquiry framework is dynamic and recursive. Each week we begin a new cycle: Immerse, Investigate, Coalesce, *repeat.* This is a dance between partners. Immerse dances solo at first, then pairs for a tango back and forth with Investigate. Then Investigate moves over to salsa with Coalesce, the inquiry tossed between them. Finally, Coalesce settles into its own creative dance space to go solo, preparing for its grand finale. All dance to the tune of poetry slams we listen to along the way. These dances are ever-shifting, depending on . . . well, everything.

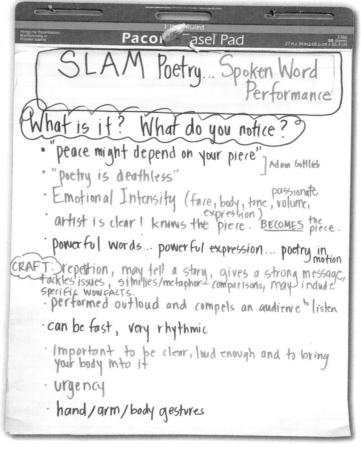

SLAM Poetry... Spoken Word Performance

What is it? What do you notice?
- "peace might depend on your piece"] Adam Gottlieb
- "poetry is deathless"
- Emotional Intensity (face, body, tone, volume, passionate expression)
- artist is clear! knows the piece. BECOMES the piece.
- powerful words... powerful expression... poetry in motion
- CRAFT: repetition, may tell a story, gives a strong message, tackles issues, similies/metaphor comparisons, may include specific WOW FACTS.
- performed outloud and compels an audience to listen
- can be fast, very rhythmic
- Important to be clear, loud enough and to bring your body into it
- urgency
- hand/arm/body gestures

Mini-Inquiry: Spotlight on the Environment

The following six pages (shown with the light green folder graphic behind the text) spotlight just one of our weeklong mini-inquiries: the environment. This close look will offer a taste of how the vision, rhythm, structure, strategies, core practices, and content blend together in a mini-inquiry. Since this one occurred at the end of the school year, the strategies and core practices we are using have been practiced again and again. Students know how to use these effectively. Although in teaching we clearly state the strategies, model our thinking and work, and guide the set up for our inquiries, we are no longer introducing or teaching *how*. At this point in the year, most of our work is comprised of deeply embedded practices.

IMMERSE

Week 5: Day 1

▶ **Discover ways people take action on an issue.**

We begin the week by watching brief videos of climate, science, and environmental marches that have taken place around the country, bringing forth what we already know and seeking to understand the various perspectives of environmental advocates. Some of these issues are familiar to the students from previous discussions, conversations with family, and experiences in their communities. We discuss: Why are people marching? What is their message? How is voice being used here? What do we know about climate change and environmental issues in general? What are we thinking? What do we wonder?

[Messages for the Earth]

Severn Cullis-Suzuki	Xiahtezcatl Roske-Martinez
• 1992 speech to the UN	• 2015 speech to the UN
• Fighting for her future	• Almost 200 countries are in the UN
• She is speaking for all youth	• Earth Guardians— a group of people protecting Earth, air, water.
• We should act as one to achieve our goal	• All life is sacred
• ECHO, a group of 12 and 13 year old activists	• Life is a gift
• "You are what you do, not what you say."	• Standing up to have a better future
• Trying to fight poverty, Earth destruction	• Disasters are occuring because of the way we live
• Traveled 5000 miles, kids raised money themselves	• The existence of my existence is at stake
• She is also speaking for generations to come	• DEMANDING to make the environment better
• Not taking action! You can't fix the destruction	• EVERYONE must take action before it is too late
	• Don't be afraid to dream big
	• The window of opportunity is closing
	• The solutions are here, we just need to use them.
	• 15 year old youth-leader.
	• We must go renewable instead of non-renewable.
	• Greed mindset of destruction is tearing apart the planet.
	• We are being called upon
	• "What better time to be born than now? What better time to be alive than now?"
	• The hope of our generation is in our hands.

After taking notes, students write reflections (see p. 239).

INVESTIGATE

Week 5: Days 2, 3, and 4

▶ **Delve into issues by reading, viewing, and responding to information.**
We read a news article about a small group of teens leading a lawsuit against the U.S. government for its inaction on climate change. Reading and annotating the article together, students continue on their own, working independently or in pairs. These questions guide their responses: What did the text say? What do you think and feel about that? What do you wonder? What feels important? What lingers? What do you notice about voice? What is our responsibility?

Next up are two videos and a double-column form for note-taking in students' lesson books. The first video is Severn Suzuki's speech to the United Nations Conference on climate in 1992 in which she speaks on behalf of the children of the world, urging adults—the U.N. delegates among them—to take better care of the world's people and its environment. As she speaks, we jot important points from her message for the Earth in the first column of a response scaffold (see p. 238). Then we view Xiuhtexcatl Roske-Martinez's (the leader of the youth lawsuit from the previously read article) 2015 speech to a United Nations conference on climate change in which he charges the assembled representatives to take action to save the planet from destruction by humans. We synthesize the essential aspects of his message in the second column.

With our double-entry notes, we compare the messages in the two speeches, turning and talking with our table groups, then sharing with the whole class. In their lesson books, students write in response to these questions: How are these two messages similar? What are you thinking and feeling about these messages? What feels most powerful or urgent to you right now?

My Thinking

When I hear Xiuhtezcatl speak, I feel VERY inspired. He first spoke when he was only SIX YEARS OLD! And now he is 16, and 2 years ago he spoke in front of the U.N.! He is the youth leader of the Earth Guardians, a group dedicated to saving our environment, planet and future and future generations. I love the environment, but I doubt as much as him. I admire Xiuhtezcatl because he and the Earth Guardians are saving and changing the planet and our futures.

My Thinking

These two messages are similar, because both of them are standing up for the earth. Both are demanding that we change our ways of dealing with environmental problems. They are both daring us to take responsibility, take action, to protect what gives us life.

▶ **Research independently.**

For homework, students explore the Earth Guardians website and use a response sheet with three simple prompts to scaffold their thinking:

1. Generally explore the website. What do you notice? What do you find interesting? What seems to be the purpose of the site?

2. Watch at least one video. What is the gist of the video? What is your thinking about what you heard and viewed? What is a question that lingers for you?

3. Click on the TAKE ACTION link at the bottom of the home page. Explore this section. List ten things that you and your family could do to take action for the Earth.

The next day, students arrive enthusiastic about their homework. This is not always the case! Guided by the response sheet, students loved the freedom to explore and were inspired by the young people powerfully speaking out in support of the environment and for future generations. Making a list of things they could do with their families to make a difference in small, everyday ways encouraged them. A call to action authentically brewed inside these students.

▶ **Summarize issues on a teaching poster.**

To investigate specific issues, students follow a link to an article on the Bill Moyers website titled "Top Climate Stories to Watch in 2017" (Gaworecki 2017). Students read the numbered, boldfaced issues and note the issues they are most drawn to. Based on their interests, kids form small investigative groups. Their task: to read the blurb about their selected issue, to jot notes and discuss the issue with their group, and then to create an informative poster to use in teaching the class about the issue.

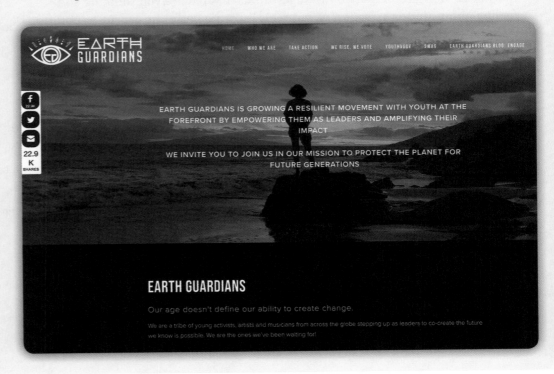

EARTH GUARDIANS

Our age doesn't define our ability to create change.

We are a tribe of young activists, artists and musicians from across the globe stepping up as leaders to co-create the future we know is possible. We are the ones we've been waiting for!

Teaching posters must have a title, succinctly state the issue, offer important points on the issue, briefly describe their thinking, list lingering questions, and include a related diagram or illustration. Eagerly, students get to work. Not all their issues are simple or easy to understand. In brief, one-on-one conferences, kids consider: What does the text say? What are you thinking?

Some students need more support to fully grasp the ideas, so we reread and discuss together. Others browse for additional information and ideas for images. They are all making connections between what they already know and what they are learning. Students discuss and sketch possible layouts for their teaching posters. In a follow-up session, they work to craft their posters and rehearse for their brief presentations.

▶ **Share and learn about various issues.**

As the small groups present, students take notes on the most important ideas of each. After each presentation, the floor is opened up to questions from the audience. They are astounded by the fact that deforestation affects climate change more than planes, trains, and automobiles combined! Kids are saddened by the fact that 2015–2016 was the most devastating year to date for our coral reefs and record-low levels for Arctic Sea ice. And then, they are puzzled by the denial of climate change by many across the country. They get a sense that this is disastrous for their future.

Students take notes as small groups present teaching posters.

COALESCE

Week 5: Day 5

▶ **Respond to the issue with art and poetry.**

Pastel chalks, white drawing paper, scrap paper, and art boards are stacked on the counter. Our social justice playlist adds energy and rhythm in the background. Today, on day 5, we express our personal responses to this week's inquiry, beginning with beloved places in nature. I say, "Think about places in nature that you have been, maybe once, maybe several times. Maybe these places are close to home, in your backyard, neighborhood, across town. Or maybe these places are further away, up in the mountains, at the ocean, in the forest, in another state, another country. Now, choose one that evokes a sense of awe, wonder, or deep appreciation, one that you love, see as beautiful, feel connected to. Close your eyes and zoom in on that place. See it. Feel it. Imagine being there."

With these images in mind, students use chalk pastels to re-create these beloved natural spaces on paper, feeling their personal connection to the Earth. I provide several images as mentor pieces for our artwork.

Later in the morning, we move into poetry. For our environmental mentor text, Prince Ea steps in through his powerful spoken-word performance of "Dear Future Generations: Sorry" on YouTube. After viewing his piece several times, students grab their writer's notebooks and pencils and head outdoors to sit in silence, to breathe in green grass and blue sky, and to make apology lists of their own. I ask them, "If you were speaking to the earth, to trees, land, animals, rivers or oceans, what would you say? If you were speaking to people, who would you be speaking to and what would you say?" Silent and subdued, everyone is deep in thought and poetic word weavings.

Sorry

I'm sorry

I'm sorry we blocked out the voice of the earth
      when we had no choice but to listen

I'm sorry you couldn't see a blue sky
      because of our greed our need for money

I'm sorry we had no solutions to fix pollution
      no one to care there were no bears

I'm sorry you could not see winter
      it was a time of year where it snowed and
      the river froze

I'm sorry we were so obsessed with cutting down trees
      we forgot that they are an essential need

I'm sorry we dumped our problems into the ocean
      Then those problems choked all the sea life
      there was to see...

I'm sorry we were too busy liking and tweeting
      We couldn't like the tweet of bluebirds

And lastly

I'm sorry that our generation was too busy to realize
      that we cannot throw away the earth

But we can always renew our mindset

And save the earth.

Dear Earth,

I'm sorry for [the] destruction of our planet

For the times when the air is so thick with pollution we can't see.

I'm sorry that my children's children's children may never get to see snow.

I'm sorry for the whale, washed up on the shore, bits of plastic inside it.

I'm sorry for the fish, choking on plastic we threw in the water, too lazy to throw it away.

I'm sorry that the landfills keep filling up, up, up.

. . . I'm sorry earth

So I ask you, is this who we are?

Weeks 6–7: Creating and Performing Poetry

Two weeks to go. Our final slam performance hovers, while fear and excitement dance inside us all. Arriving at this moment, we have cycled through four mini-inquires—the Women's Movement, LGBTQ issues, Othering, and Environment—but mini only in length. Arriving on this Monday, we are full, overflowing, ready for the final, courageous leap into the power of our own voices being heard.

TAKE PUBLIC

■ Create slam poems and prepare for performance.

All along we have been preparing for this leap.

Alongside our work with issues, we have been studying slam poetry. Each week, as our understanding of this form grows, our poetry has taken on the energetic, emotional, edgy voice of slam. To support these voices, we play with breath, vocal, and memorization practices. We unwind our nervous systems and practice putting our voices into the circle. Memorizing lines from our poems, we stimulate the memory muscles in our brains. These practices become daily warm-ups. Deepening our experience with this form, we welcome a local slam artist to our classroom. Listening to our first live slam performance, we begin to imagine ourselves standing in that performance space.

These next two weeks are dedicated to our practice. Through our practice, we revise our rhythm and our words. Our peers offer feedback and encouragement. We cultivate the courage and determination to be heard. Daily, we meet with partners, small groups, the walls, our whole class. Students blossom along with their performances.

First, there is Oliver. One morning, we gather in a standing circle to recite whichever mantras or lines from our poems we had memorized for the previous night's homework. This is a first go at memorizing. Just a phrase or sentence is expected. Some are meaningful, "I am grateful for today. I am grateful for my family. I am grateful for my life." Others are quite simple, "I like books." All are brief. Except Oliver's. Out of his mouth pour powerful words that sound like the beginning of an intense book.

> So I try
> To step into the shoes
> Of a young boy fleeing war
> With only a ripped up bag
> And a 40-year-old mother
> Then I realize he has no shoes to protect his feet
> From the coldness of the Earth.
> He runs from bombs
> Only to be stopped by border patrol
> But his bare feet go on.
> After, his mother is beaten
> "Stay strong," she whispers
> In her cold dying voice . . .

I have goosebumps. "What is that from?" I ask.
"My slam," he responds.
"Wait. You wrote that?"
"Yep," he hesitantly beams.

Then, there is Juliana. As we immerse ourselves into practice with each other, her fear of being vulnerable, of being heard in such a personal way, heightens. She hesitates to speak more than a line or two in front of an audience. Peers cheer her on, suggest ways to get over the humps, break through her blocks. Then, one day, she realizes that as a ballet dancer, she doesn't fear the stage. And so, she begins to move with her words. And out they flow, to the great cheers of her classmates.

VIDEO CLIP

Teacher and students reflect on poetry and performance.

Students perform slam poetry.

And then, Anya. Stepping into slam is a natural place for her to be. With each word, she owns it, believes it, becomes it. She sounds ready to take on the world and its injustices with her sassy hip sway, sweeping hand gestures, and sincere, pointed questions. "Bring it on!" she seems to say beneath it all.

> "Everyone is treated equally."
> "No one is left out."
> These are the false messages we are given
> To believe and never question
> But under all the layers of protection
> They hide from us
> The Truth . . .

Finally, Nailah. I sense her questioning the world, challenging the way we see and believe. In our practice sessions, she works with a poem for the Earth. Then one day, a different slam emerges at home, something real, relevant, alive.

> Mom I say
> the world spoke to me today
> not him not her but me
> she called for help
> with a yelp she said
> her trees are being cut down
> and her soul is about to drown
> in the deep blue sea
> where there is nothing left to be
> and what do you say?
> you say money gas oil
> that I have to pay . . .
> . . . mother I say
> the world spoke to me today.

Two days to go. Dress rehearsal. Fresh anticipation runs through the room. One after the other, students put out their slams to the whole class as audience for the first time. Rough patches and forgotten lines, start-overs and turn-up-the-volume reminders, and spine tingles and goosebumps, mouth drops and teared-up eyes. Ready.

■ Perform our slams.

Zero days to go. Today, we slam. Students arrive, equally anxious and excited. With backpacks tucked away, we gather in circle to breathe and warm up our voices together. We step into our places as parents arrive.

As each child steps courageously forth, all the students become pillars of strength and determination for each other. Oliver invites the audience to tears. Juliana is in tears. Anya nails it, twice, and Nailah brings on the intensity for all. Every child rises to her or his best slam moment ever. Heartfelt cheers, whoops, and hollers ring out again and again. Parents become witness to the journey and the transformation unfolding before them. Today, we slam for social justice and the environment. We slam for ourselves and each other. We slam to feel, to create, to embody, to express, to stand up, to offer our voices. Together, we rise.

And so, we bring to a close this journey of inquiry and are forever changed. For this is the true purpose of what we do each day in the classroom. Is it not?

Step Through the Door

I am an immigrant
I am equal
I am an unstoppable force
      However for some reason
People keep stopping me.

After I was rejected something clearly
Expected because for a reason
People like teasen
A person of color.

A person that now wants
To be duller
Because of a phone call
Because of an answer.

I say hello
They say goodbye
I say I need a place
They say that's not the case because
It's a maze for people of color
And now I am duller
Because of some words

Now I'm a bird ready to fly
Ready to cry
Because I am different
But, I am now a booming human
I am now a sequel of equal
I have now stepped through the door.

Works Cited

Professional Resources

Adichie, Chimanda Ngozi. "The Danger of a Single Story." https://www.ted.com/talks/chimamanda_adichie_the_danger_of_a_single_story.

Allington, Richard. 2002. "What I've Learned About Effective Reading Instruction from a Decade of Studying Exemplary Elementary Classroom Teachers." *Phi Delta Kappan* 83 (10): 740–47.

———. 2012. *What Really Matters for Struggling Readers: Designing Researched-Based Programs*. 3rd ed. Boston: Pearson.

Atwell, Nancie. *In the Middle: A Lifetime of Learning About Writing, Reading, and Adolescents*. 4th ed. Portsmouth, NH: Heinemann.

Bain, Robert B. 2007. "They Thought the World Was Flat? Applying the Principles of How People Learn in Teaching High School History." In *How Students Learn: History in the Classroom*, ed. M. Suzanne Donovan and John Bransford. Washington, DC: National Academies Press.

Bennett, Samantha. 2007. *That Workshop Book: New Systems and Structures for Classrooms That Read, Write, and Think*. Portsmouth, NH: Heinemann.

Bomer, Katherine. 2016. *The Journey Is Everything: Teaching Essays That Students Want to Write for People Who Want to Read Them*. Portsmouth, NH: Heinemann.

Britton, James. 1970. *Language and Learning: The Importance of Speech in Children's Development*. Hammondsworth, UK: Penguin.

Bruner, Jerome. 2009. *The Process of Education*. Rev. ed. Cambridge, MA: Harvard University Press.

Buhrow, Brad, and Anne Upczak Garcia. 2006. *Ladybugs, Tornadoes, and Swirling Galaxies: English Language Learners Discover Their World Through Inquiry*. Portland, ME: Stenhouse.

Burns, Ken, dir. 2009. *The National Parks: America's Best Idea*. TV Miniseries, 6 episodes, 2 hours. Production Companies: Florentine Productions and WETA. Distributed by PBS (TV) and PBS Home Video (Video).

Cazden, Courtney. 2001. *Classroom Discourse: The Language of Teaching and Learning*. Portsmouth, NH: Heinemann.

Cervetti, C. Jaynes, and E. Hiebert. 2009. "Increasing Opportunities to Acquire Knowledge Through Reading." In *Reading More, Reading Better*, ed. E. Hiebert. New York: Guilford.

Colorado Public Radio. "Boulder 5th Graders Find Hope, Yes Hope, in the 2016 Election." https://bit.ly/2enUENA.

Daniels, Harvey. 2017. *The Curious Classroom*. Portsmouth, NH: Heinemann.

Engel, Susan. 2011. "Children's Need to Know: Curiosity in Schools." *Harvard Educational Review* 81 (4): 625–45.

Fielding, Linda, and P. David Pearson. 1994. "Reading Comprehension: What Works?" *Educational Leadership* 51 (5): 62–67.

Gaworski, Mike. 2017. "Top Climate Stories to Watch in 2017." https://billmoyers.com/story/top-climate-stories-watch-2017/.

Goudvis, Anne, and Stephanie Harvey. *Toolkit Texts American History: Short Nonfiction for Teaching History*. Portsmouth, NH: Heinemann.

Graves, Donald. 1991. *Build a Literate Classroom*. Portsmouth, NH: Heinemann.

Harvey, Stephanie. 1998. *Nonfiction Matters: Reading, Writing, and Researching, Grades 3–5*. Portland, ME: Stenhouse.

Harvey, Stephanie, and Harvey Daniels. 2015. *Comprehension and Collaboration*, revised ed. Portsmouth, NH: Heinemann.

Harvey, Stephanie, and Anne Goudvis. 2016a. *The Primary Comprehension Toolkit: Language and Lessons for K–2.* 2nd ed. Portsmouth, NH: Heinemann.

———. 2016b. *The Intermediate Comprehension Toolkit: Language and Lessons for Active Literacy.* 2nd ed. Portsmouth, NH: Heinemann.

———. 2017. *Strategies That Work: Teaching Comprehension for Engagement, Understanding and Building Knowledge.* 3rd ed. Portland, ME: Stenhouse.

Harvey, Stephanie, and Annie Ward. 2017. *From Striving to Thriving: How to Grow Confident, Capable Readers.* New York: Scholastic.

Harwayne, Shelley. 1999. *Going Public: Priorities and Practice at the Manhattan New School.* Portsmouth, NH: Heinemann.

———. 2001. *Writing Through Childhood: Rethinking Process and Product.* Portsmouth, NH: Heinemann.

Heard, Georgia. 2016. *Heart Maps: Helping Students Create and Craft Authentic Writing.* Portsmouth, NH: Heinemann.

Heisey, Natalie, and Linda Kucan. 2010. "Introducing Science Concepts to Primary Students Through Read-Alouds: Interactions and Multiple Texts Make the Difference." *The Reading Teacher* 63 (8): 666–76. doi:10.1598/RT.63.8.5

Johnston, Peter. 2004. *Choice Words: How Our Language Affects Children's Learning.* Portland, ME: Stenhouse.

———. 2012. *Opening Minds: Using Language to Change Lives.* Portland, ME: Stenhouse.

Keene, Ellin. 2018. *Engaging Children: Igniting a Drive for Deeper Learning.* Portsmouth, NH: Heinemann.

Krashen, Stephen D., Sy-Ying Lee, Christy Lao. 2017. *Comprehensible and Compelling: The Causes and Effects of Free Voluntary Reading.* Santa Barbara, CA: Libraries Unlimited.

Lamb, Annette, and Daniel Callison. 2012. *Graphic Inquiry.* Denver, CO: Libraries Unlimited.

Levstik, Linda S., and Keith Barton. 2001. *Doing History: Investigating with Children in Elementary and Middle Schools.* Mahwah, NJ: Lawrence Erlbaum.

Logan, Barbara. The Curiosity Coma. www.efficacy.org/resources/the-curiosity-coma/.

Mehan, Hugh. 1979. *Learning Lessons: Social Organization in the Classroom.* Cambridge, MA: Harvard University Press.

McTighe, Jay, and Grant Wiggins. 2013. "Essential Questions." http://www.ascd.org/publications/books/109004/chapters/what-makes-a-question-essential%A2.aspx.

Miller, Debbie. 2013. *Reading with Meaning: Teaching Comprehension in the Primary Grades.* 2nd ed. Portland, ME: Stenhouse.

———. 2018. *What's the Best That Could Happen? New Possibilities for Teachers and Readers.* Portsmouth, NH: Heinemann.

Mohr, Kathleen, and Eric Mohr. 2007. "Extending English Learners' Classroom Interactions Using the Response Protocol." *The Reading Teacher* 60 (5): 440–50.

Murdoch, Kath. 2015. *The Power of Inquiry: Teaching and Learning with Curiosity, Creativity, and Purpose in the Contemporary Classroom.* Melbourne, AU: Seastar Education.

Nichols, M. 2006. *Comprehension Through Conversation: The Power of Purposeful Talk in the Reading Workshop.* Portsmouth, NH: Heinemann.

Patterson, Katherine. 1995. *A Sense of Wonder: On Reading and Writing Books for Children.* New York: Plume.

Pearson, P. David. 2006. Letter to the Editor. *New York Times,* March 28.

Pianta, Robert C., Jay Belsky, Renate Houts, Fred Morrison, and NICHD. 2007. "Teaching Opportunities in America's Elementary Classrooms." *Science* 315 (5820): 1795–96.

Ray, Katie Wood. 2010. *In Pictures and in Words: Teaching the Qualities of Good Writing Through Illustration Study.* Portsmouth, NH: Heinemann.

Richhart, Ron. 2012. "The Real Power of Questions." *Creative Teaching and Learning* 2 (4): 8–12.

———. 2015. *Creating Cultures of Thinking: The Eight Forces We Must Master to Truly Transform Our Schools.* San Francisco: Jossey-Bass.

Rubin, Laurie. 2013. *To Look Closely: Science and Literacy in the Natural World.* Portland, ME: Stenhouse.

Saunders, William, and Claude Goldenberg. 2007. "The Effects of Instructional Conversation in English Learners' Concepts of Friendship and Story Comprehension." In *Talking Texts: How Speech and Writing Interact in School Learning*, ed. Rosalind Horowitz, 221–52. Mahwah, NJ: Erlbaum.

Smith, Frank. 1987. *Joining the Literacy Club: Further Essays into Education*. Portsmouth, NH: Heinemann.

Stead, Tony. 2005. *Reality Checks: Teaching Reading Comprehension with Nonfiction, K–5*. Portland, ME: Stenhouse.

Stipek, Deborah J. 2002. *Motivation to Learn: Theory to Practice*, 4th ed. Needham Heights, MA: Allyn and Bacon.

Tishman, Shari, David N. Perkins, and Eileen Jay. 1995. *The Thinking Classroom: Learning and Teaching in a Culture of Thinking*. Boston: Allyn and Bacon.

Vinton, Vicki. 2018. *Dynamic Teaching for Deeper Reading*. Portsmouth, NH: Heinemann.

Volpat, James. 2009. *Writing Circles: Kids Revolutionize Workshop*. Portsmouth, NH: Heinemann.

Vygotsky, Lev. 1978. Mind in Society: The Development of Higher Psychological Processes. Boston: Harvard University Press.

Children's Literature

Andrews, Troy. 2015. *Trombone Shorty*. New York: Harry N. Abrams.

Bandy, Michael S., and Eric Stein. 2015. *Granddaddy's Turn: A Journey to the Ballot Box*. Somerville, MA: Candlewick Press.

Borenstein, Seth. 2014. "Study: Polar Bears Disappearing from Key Region." *Associated Press*, November 17.

Brown, Don. 1999. *Rare Treasure: Mary Anning and Her Remarkable Discoveries*. Boston: Houghton Mifflin.

Brown, Peter. 2009. *The Curious Gardener*. New York: Little, Brown.

Brummel, Bill, dir. 2015. *Selma: The Bridge to the Ballot*. Bill Brummel Productions, Inc. 40 mins. Dolby Digital. Distributed by Teaching Tolerance.

Buss, Fran Leeper, with Daisy Cubias. 1991. *Journey of the Sparrows*. New York: Puffin Books.

Campoy, F. Isabel, and Theresa Howell. 2016. *Maybe Something Beautiful: How Art Transformed a Neighborhood*. Boston: HMH Book for Young Readers.

Cassino, Mark. 2009. *The Story of Snow: The Science of Winter's Wonder*. San Francisco: Chronicle Books.

Conkling, Winifred. 2011. *Sylvia and Aki*. New York: Yearling Books.

Cousteau, Philippe, and Deborah Hopkinson. 2016. *Follow the Moon Home: A Tale of One Idea, Twenty Kids, and a Hundred Sea Turtles*. San Francisco: Chronicle.

Dallas, Sandra. 2015. *Red Berries, White Clouds, Blue Sky*. Ann Arbor, MI: Sleeping Bear Press.

Davies, Jacqueline. 2004. *The Boy Who Drew Birds: A Story of John James Audubon*. Boston: Houghton Mifflin.

Ea, Prince. 2015. "I Am NOT Black, You Are NOT White." https://www.youtube.com/watch?v=q0qD2K2RWkc.

Ellis, Deborah. 2001. *The Breadwinner*. Oxford, UK: Oxford University Press.

French, S. Terrell. 2011. *Operation Redwood*. New York: Amulet Books.

Hill, Laban Carrick. 2013. *When the Beat Was Born: DJ Cool Herc and the Creation of Hip-Hop*. New York: Roaring Brook Press.

Jones, Jacqueline, Peter H. Wood, Thomas Borstelmann, Elaine Tyler May, and Vicki L. Ruiz. 2013. *Created Equal: A History of the United States*. Boston: Pearson.

Kadohata, Cynthia. 2009. *Weedflower*. New York: Atheneum Books for Young Readers.

Kalman, Bobbie. 2009. *Japan the Land*. St. Catherines, ON: Crabtree Publishing.

Lai, Thanhha. 2011. *Inside Out and Back Again*. New York: HarperCollins Children's Books.

Leedy, Loreen. 2010. *The Shocking Truth About Energy*. New York: Holiday House.

Lord, Bette Bao. 2003. *The Year of the Boar and Jackie Robinson*. New York: HarperCollins.

Lowery, Lynda Blackmon. 2015. *Turning 15 on the Road to Freedom: My Story of the 1965 Selma Voting Rights March*. New York: Speak.

Lyon, George Ella. "Where I Come From" (poem)

Malaspina, Ann. 2012. *Heart on Fire: Susan B. Anthony Votes for President*. Park Ridge, IL: Albert Whitman & Company.

Markel, Michelle. 2013. *Brave Girl: Clara and the Shirtwaist Makers' Strike of 1909*. New York: Balzer & Bray.

Markle, Sandra. 2006. *Little Lost Bat*. Watertown, MA: Charlesbridge.

———. 2012. *Waiting for Ice*. Watertown, MA: Charlesbridge.

Martin, Jacqueline Briggs. 1998. *Snowflake Bentley*. New York: Houghton Mifflin Harcourt.

Messner, Kate. 2011. *Over and Under the Pond*. San Francisco: Chronicle.

Milson, Andrew. 2013. *Grand Canyon National Park. Ladders* Social Studies 5. Washington, DC: National Geographic.

Nardo, Don. 2014. *The Split History of the Women's Suffrage Movement*. North Mankato, MN: Compass Point Books.

National Geographic Wild. 2017. *Polar Bear 101* (video clip: 3:42 mins.). Angeli Gabriel, producer/narrator. https://video.nationalgeographic.com/video/101-videos/0000015e-3e23-db02-a9df-3eb716d90000.

Navasky, Bruno. 1993. *Festival in My Heart: Poems by Japanese Children*. New York: Harry N. Abrams.

National Geographic School Pub. 2012. "The Power of Speech." National Geographic *Ladders Reading/Language Arts*. Boston: Cengage Learning.

Newman, Mark. 2015. *Polar Bears*. New York: Henry Holt.

"On Thin Ice," *National Geographic Explorer*. 2007.

Oswald, Nancy. 2008. *Hard Face Moon*. Palmer Lake, CO: Filter Press.

Paterson, Katherine. 1990. *The Tale of the Mandarin Ducks*. New York: Puffin Unicorn Books.

Polonsky, Ami. 2016. *Gracefully Grayson*. New York: Hyperion.

Pough, Frederick H. 1988. *A Field Guide to Rocks and Minerals*. Boston: Houghton Mifflin.

Roske-Martinez, Xiuhtexcatl. 2015. "Xiuhtezcatl, Indigenous Climate Activist at the United Nations Conference on Climate Change." https://www.youtube.com/watch?v=27gtZ1oV4kw.

Ryan, Pam Muñoz. 2000. *Esperañza Rising*. New York: Scholastic.

———. 2002. *When Marian Sang: The True Recital of Marian Anderson*. New York: Scholastic.

Ryder, Joanne. 2000. *Each Living Thing*. Orlando, FL: Gulliver Books.

Stone, Tanya Lee. 2010. *Elizabeth Leads the Way: Elizabeth Cady Stanton and the Right to Vote*. New York: Square Fish.

Suzuki, Severn. 1992. Speech to United Nations Conference on climate in 1992. https://www.youtube.com/watch?v=oJJGuIZVfLM.

Thompson, Laurie Ann. 2015. *Emmanuel's Dream: The True Story of Emmanuel Ofosu Yeboah*. New York: Schwartz & Wade Books.

Tomecek, Steve, and Carsten Peter. 2011. *Everything Rocks and Minerals*. Washington, DC: National Geographic Kids.

Tonatiuh, Duncan. 2014. *Separate Is Never Equal: Sylvia Mendez and Her Family's Fight for Desegregation*. New York: Harry N. Abrams/Abrams Books for Young Readers.

Williams-Garcia, Rita. 2011. *One Crazy Summer*. New York: Amistad.

Winter, Jeanette. 2008. *Wangari's Trees of Peace: A True Story from Africa*. New York: Harcourt Children's Books.

———. 2009. *Nasreen's Secret School: A True Story from Afghanistan*. New York: Beach Lane Books.

———. 2014. *Malala, a Brave Girl from Pakistan/Iqbal, a Brave Boy from Pakistan: Two Stories of Bravery*. New York: Beach Lane Books.

Winter, Jonah. 2015. *Lillian's Right to Vote: A Celebration of the Voting Rights Act of 1965*. New York: Schwartz & Bray Books.

Yashima, Taro. [1955] 1983. *Crow Boy*. New York: Puffin Books.

Credits for borrowed material continued from p. ii

Image credits